Certified macromedia® DREAMWEAVER® 4 Developer Study Guide

Ben Forta with Robert Crooks, Sue Hove, and Jay Kellett

macromedia® PRESS

This title is published by Macromedia Press in association with Que Publishing.

www.quepublishing.com

201 West 103rd Street, Indianapolis, Indiana 46290

Certified Macromedia© 4 Dreamweaver™ Developer Study Guide

International Standard Book Number: 0-7897-2736-6

Library of Congress Catalog Card Number: 2002100460

Printed in the United States of America

First Printing: March 2002

04 03 02 4 3 2 1

Trademarks

Warning and Disclaimer

Publisher
David Culverwell

Executive Editor
Candace Hall

Acquisitions Editor
Angela Kozlowski

Development Editor
Mark Kozlowski

Managing Editor
Thomas F. Hayes

Senior Editor
Susan Ross Moore

Copy Editor
Barbara Hacha

Indexer
Mandie Frank

Proofreader
Linda Seifert

Technical Editor
Glenda Vigoreaux

Team Coordinator
Cindy Teeters

Interior Designer
Anne Jones

Cover Designer
Alan Clements

Page Layout
Michelle Mitchell

Contents at a Glance

Table of Contents

About the Authors

Ben Forta is Macromedia, Inc.'s Senior Product Evangelist and has almost 20 years of experience in the computer industry in product development, support, training, and product marketing. Ben is the author of the best-selling *ColdFusion Web Application Construction Kit* (now in its fourth edition), as well as books on SQL, JavaServer Pages, Macromedia HomeSite, Macromedia Spectra, WAP, Windows 2000, and more. Ben coauthored the official ColdFusion training courses, writes regular columns on ColdFusion and Internet development, and now spends a considerable amount of time lecturing and speaking on Internet-related technologies. Born in London, England and educated in London, New York, and Los Angeles, Ben now lives in Oak Park, Michigan with his wife, Marcy, and their six children. Ben welcomes your e-mail at `ben@forta.com` and invites you to visit his Web site at `http://www.forta.com/`.

Robert Crooks is the Technical Lead for Macromedia Educational Services and coauthor of the Macromedia authorized training courses Fast Track to Dreamweaver and Advanced Dreamweaver Techniques. He also contributed to the Macromedia Dreamweaver 4 Certified Developer Exam. He has been an active user of Dreamweaver since version 1.

Sue Hove is Macromedia, Inc.'s Director of Instructor Readiness for its Education Services department. She has more than 15 years of experience in the computer industry in application design and programming, relational databases, training, and course development. She has applied her applications development and training expertise for software vendors such as Informix, Powersoft/Sybase, and Allaire/Macromedia. For the past five years, she has been shaping Macromedia's curriculum by writing and delivering its training course offerings and certifying other instructors to teach Macromedia's courses worldwide. She coauthored Macromedia's Fast Track to Dreamweaver and Advanced Dreamweaver Techniques courses along with two other authors. Sue now lives in Holmes, Pennsylvania and welcomes your e-mail at `sue@hove.com`.

Jay Kellett is the principal of Blue Box Software (`http://www.blueboxsw.com`), which specializes in business-education solutions. He coauthored the official Macromedia Dreamweaver training courses and teaches a variety of technology courses. Since graduating with a Masters of Science in Instructional Technology from Bloomsburg University in 1994, he has completed projects for a variety of large and small companies, including PriceWaterhouseCoopers, Merck, and the FDIC.

Dedication

To Kalpana, who put up with yet a few more of my endless hours in front of the computer to write this. —Robert Crooks

To Mom, Dad, Chris, Sonya, the Sheas in Boston, the Levesques in California, and one martini-drinking grandmother in Whiting, New Jersey. You know who you are. —Jay Kellett

Acknowledgments

Thanks to Robert Crooks, Sue Hove, and Jay Kellet, who did all the actual writing for this title. Thanks to everyone on the Macromedia certification team for providing the authors with material and information when needed. And thanks to Angela Kozlowski and all at Que and Macromedia Press for putting together yet another best-seller-to-be. *—Ben Forta*

Many thanks to Angela Kozlowski of Que Publishing, who managed to keep this project on track without making it painful, and to Sue Hove, who not only answers e-mail at any time of the day or night, but always manages to make me laugh with her replies. *—Robert Crooks*

Sue would like to acknowledge her co-authors, Robert and Jay, for teaching her everything she knows about Dreamweaver. It's been great working with you guys, on the courseware and on this book. I look forward to working on many more projects together. And to Ben Forta, for letting me get involved in the writing process and believing in me…again. *—Sue Hove*

Thanks to Ben, Sue, and Robert—a set of fantastic collaborators. And to the many great people at Macromedia and Macromedia Press, without whom we would have nothing to write about and no one to print it. Thanks also to the many great clients with whom I've gotten the chance to teach, learn from, work for, bill, and occasionally drink with: Matt Meyer, Todd Harris, Rich Wein, Ed Rodrigo, John Olszewski, Jim Wetzel, Shawn Milheim, Pete Meyers, Jervis Thompson, Adam Peterson, Rick Kauffman, and Bob Kelly. And finally, thanks to people who make it all worth it: Nicole, Moosh, Jimx, Todd, Ed, Randy, Angel, Chaz, Ken, and Mary. *—Jay Kellet*

Tell Us What You Think!

As the reader of this book, *you* are our most important critic and commentator. We value your opinion and want to know what we're doing right, what we could do better, what areas you'd like to see us publish in, and any other words of wisdom you're willing to pass our way.

As an acquisitions editor for Macromedia Press, I welcome your comments. You can fax, e-mail, or write me directly to let me know what you did or didn't like about this book—as well as what we can do to make our books stronger.

Please note that I cannot help you with technical problems related to the topic of this book, and that due to the high volume of mail I receive, I might not be able to reply to every message.

When you write, please be sure to include this book's title and author as well as your name and phone or fax number. I will carefully review your comments and share them with the author and editors who worked on the book.

Fax: 510-524-2221

E-mail: `ask@peachpit.com`

Mail: Angela Kozlowski
Macromedia Press
1240 Eighth Street
Berkeley, CA 94710
USA

INTRODUCTION

Macromedia's Web tools are well known and widely used. The idea of a certification method to ensure that Web developers are confident and competent with these tools is a logical move, especially because many people now style themselves as Web design experts. Macromedia's Dreamweaver is one of the most widely used tools for creating Web pages and sites and is a good candidate for a certification test.

With the development of the Dreamweaver certification exam, a similar study guide was inevitable. Even Dreamweaver experts do not use every feature of the product or tackle every Web site development problem every day; thus they will want to spend some time reviewing before the exam. The content of this study guide includes what you need to know about Dreamweaver, not only to assure yourself that you are well versed in the product and technologies for Web site development, but also to ensure that you are ready to move on to the certification process.

The subject of a Dreamweaver study guide was tackled first by looking at the overall Dreamweaver product and the tasks developers carry out with it and then delving into the details. In this book you do not find an exhaustive study of every Dreamweaver feature or every client-side Web technology. You also do not find lots of tutorials and lengthy code examples. What you find is a concise summary of the salient features of Dreamweaver, arranged in order of increasing complexity, with short code samples to provide examples of HTML, CSS, and JavaScript that a professional Dreamweaver developer should understand. You can learn how to use Dreamweaver from this book, but the idea is to reinforce and complement your experience with a summary of the features and capabilities.

As you read through the book, it may be tempting to skip certain chapters. Although you may feel confident that you know all about a particular subject, you will find many tips and notes, as well as helpful information on limitations, of which you may not be aware. These could crop up in the certification test, so starting from the beginning of this book and taking time to go through the pages in order is recommended. Of course, you can jump about all you want, but you should skim each chapter for important points (tips, cautions, and notes) prior to writing the test.

We hope you find this book useful, encapsulating a wide variety of information in a succinct format. Good luck on the certification test!

What Is the Certified Dreamweaver Developer Exam?

The popularity of Macromedia's products continues to grow, and along with it, so has the demand for experienced developers. Once upon a time (Internet time, that is, and actually not that long ago in conventional time), claiming to be a Dreamweaver developer was easy; the product was simple enough that, with a minimal investment of time and energy, developers could realistically consider themselves experts.

This is not the case anymore. The product line has grown both in actual products and in their complexity, and the levels of expertise and experience among developers are diverse. Claiming to be an expert is not that easy, and recognizing legitimate expertise is even harder.

The Macromedia Certified Professional Program

This is where certification comes into play. Formal, official certification by Macromedia helps to mark a threshold that explicitly separates developers by their knowledge and experience, making it possible to identify who is who.

The Certified Dreamweaver Developer certification is one in a series of certification tracks from Macromedia—this one concentrating on developers using Macromedia's Dreamweaver. Other exams and certification programs being developed concentrate on other products and areas of expertise.

Reasons to Get Certified

There's really only one important reason for Dreamweaver developers to become certified (aside from the goodies you'll receive): Being able to call yourself a Macromedia Certified Dreamweaver Developer means that you can command the respect and recognition that goes along with being one of the best at what you do.

Just as has happened with other products and technologies in the Web development realm, certification is likely to become a prerequisite for employers—an additional barometer by which to measure the potential of candidates and applicants.

Whether being certified helps you find a new (or better) job, helps persuade your boss that the pay raise you want is justified, helps you find new clients, or gets you listed on Macromedia's Web site so that you can attract new work or prospects—whatever the reason, it will help you stand out from the crowd.

About the Exam

Becoming a Certified Dreamweaver Developer involves being examined on your knowledge of Dreamweaver and related technologies. As far as exams go, this one is not easy—nor should it be. In fact, more than a third of all examinees fail their first test. This is not a bad thing; on the contrary, this is a good thing because it means that you really have to know your stuff to pass. You do not merely receive a paper certificate; the exam and subsequent certification have real value and real significance. "Very challenging but fair" is how many examinees describe the exam itself.

The Exam Itself

The exam is a set of multiple-choice or true-false questions you answer electronically. A computer application issues the test to you, and you'll know whether you passed immediately upon test completion.

In the test, you are presented with each question and the possible answers. Some questions have a single correct answer, whereas others have two or more (you'll be told how many answers to provide). If a question stumps you, you can skip it and come back to it later.

After you have answered all the questions, you can review them to check your answers. After you are done (or when the time is up—the test has a 60-minute time limit), you'll get your results. You need at least 70% correct to pass and achieve certification. To stand out from the crowd, you need to know your stuff and know it well. If you do not pass, you need to wait at least 30 days before you can try taking the test again. You may take the test no more than three times in a single year, starting from the date of your first test.

What You'll Be Tested On

Being a Dreamweaver expert requires that you know more than only Dreamweaver. As such, the exam includes questions on related technologies. The subjects you'll be tested on are the following:

- Design, project requirements, and usability techniques
- Implementation and coding
- Solution testing, deployment, and maintenance

Every question counts, and you cannot assume that one particular topic is more or less significant than others.

Preparing for the Exam

The most important preparation for the exam, of course, is the use of Dreamweaver itself. If you do not use Dreamweaver regularly or have not done so for an extended period, you probably will not pass the exam.

However, many experienced Dreamweaver developers still find the exam challenging. Usually, they say it is so because they don't use some features and technologies or because they have learned the product but have never paid attention to changing language and feature details (and thus are not using the product as effectively as they could be).

That is where this book fits in. This book is not a cheat sheet. It will not teach you Dreamweaver from scratch, nor will it give you a list of things to remember to pass the test. What it will do is help you systematically review every major (and not so major) feature and technology in the product—everything that you need to know to pass the test.

Where to Take the Exam

To offer the exams worldwide in as many locations as possible, Macromedia has partnered with a company called VUE. VUE offers exams and certification programs for a wide range of companies and products and has more than 2,500 regional testing facilities in more than 100 countries.

You can take the Macromedia Dreamweaver 4 Developer exam in any VUE testing center. For a current list of locations, visit the Web site:

http://www.vue.com/macromedia/

How Much It Costs

The fee to take the exam in North America is $100 (U.S.). Pricing in other countries varies. The fee must be paid at the time you register for the exam. If you need to cancel, you must do so at least 24 hours before the exam, or the fee will not be refunded.

As a special gift to readers of this book, and to encourage you to study appropriately for the test, Macromedia has sponsored a coupon that you can use for a discount off the exam fee. Refer to the coupon for details and usage information.

How to Use This Book

This book is designed to be used in two ways:

- To prepare for your exam, you should start at the beginning of the book and systematically work your way through it. The book flow and layout have been especially designed to make reviewing content as pleasant an experience as possible. The content has been designed to be highly readable and digestible in small, bite-sized chunks so that it will feel more like reading than studying.
- After you have reviewed all content, reread the topics that you feel you need extra help brushing up on. Topics are all covered in highly focused and very manageable chapters so that you can easily drill down to the exact content you need. Extensive cross-referencing enables you to read up on related topics as needed.

After the exam, you'll find that the style and design of this book makes it an invaluable desktop reference tool as well.

Contents

The book is divided into eight parts, each containing a set of highly focused chapters. Each chapter concludes with a summary and sample questions (the answers to which are in Appendix A).

Part I: Getting Started

This part covers the basics of using the Dreamweaver environment, creating sites, site and page design, and page properties. It includes chapters on the following topics:

- Web Basics
- Using the Macromedia Dreamweaver Interface
- Creating a Local Site
- Design Basics
- Page Properties

Part II: Building Web Sites

This part covers the tasks and technologies involved in building Web sites, including page layout, basic HTML content, graphics and links, frames, forms, and cascading style sheets. Chapters look at the following:

- Using Layers for Page Layout
- Using Tables for Page Layout
- Adding Basic Content
- Using Graphics
- Linking Pages and Sites
- Importing External Content
- Adding Interactivity Using Forms
- Partitioning Interfaces Using Frames
- Formatting with Cascading Style Sheets

Part III: Reuse, Collaboration, and Automation

This part covers the features built in to Dreamweaver to enable reuse of code, team collaboration, and automation through JavaScript and DHTML. It includes chapters on the following topics:

- Site Assets
- Libraries and Extensions
- Using Templates
- Server-side Includes
- Using Behaviors
- Team Collaboration

Part IV: Testing and Deployment

This part covers the testing, deployment, and maintenance of Web sites and includes chapters on the following topics:

- Testing Web Sites
- Transferring Files to Servers

Conventions Used in This Book

The people at Que Publishing have spent many years developing and publishing computer books designed for ease of use and containing the most up-to-date information available. With that experience, we've learned what features help you the most. Look for these features throughout the book to help enhance your learning experience and get the most out of Dreamweaver.

- Screen messages, code listings, and command samples appear in `monospace type`.
- Uniform Resource Locators (URLs) used to identify pages on the Web and values for Dreamweaver attributes also appear in `monospace type`.
- Terms that are defined in the text appear in *italic*. Italic type is sometimes used for emphasis, too.

TIPS

Tips give you advice on quick or overlooked procedures, including shortcuts.

NOTES

Notes present useful or interesting information that isn't necessarily essential to the current discussion but that might augment your understanding with background material or advice relating to the topic.

CAUTION

Cautions warn you about potential problems a procedure might cause, unexpected results, or mistakes that could prove costly.

- Cross-references are designed to point you to other locations in this book that provide supplemental or supporting information. Cross-references appear as follows:

→ Page layout is covered in detail in Chapter 6, "Using Layers for Page Layout," and Chapter 7, "Using Tables for Page Layout."

Where to Go from Here

Now you're ready to get started. If you think you're ready for the exam, start with the sample questions (in the book or online) to verify your skills. If you're not ready (or if the sample questions indicate that you might not be as ready as you thought), make sure that you pay attention to the topics that need more attention by reading the documentation and actually writing appropriate applications.

When you're ready, work through this book to review the content and prepare for the exam itself as described here.

And with that, we wish you good luck!

PART I

GETTING STARTED

CHAPTER 1

Web Basics

The Basics

Macromedia Dreamweaver is a tool for developing Web sites and pages. Unlike code editors, such as HomeSite, Dreamweaver is a visual editor that allows you to edit pages in an interface similar to a word processor. A Code view also allows you to modify the code directly if you need to.

Dreamweaver is the best visual editor available, not only because it is easy to use, but it also produces clean code that adheres to World Wide Web Consortium specifications, even if you edit a page many times.

To use Dreamweaver effectively, you need to understand what the World Wide Web is and how it works. In this chapter, we will review basic Web terminology and technologies.

The Internet

The Internet is a huge global network linking millions of computers and other devices. At the most basic level, the Internet allows data transfer between computers through the two-part protocol called Transmission Control Protocol/Internet Protocol (TCP/IP).

The two parts of the TCP/IP protocol have different, complementary functions:

- IP provides a way of moving data packets and a system of unique addresses on the network to make accurate delivery of data possible.
- TCP provides a way of testing the success of data packet delivery.

IP addresses are numerical, four sets of digits in groups of up to three digits, and punctuated by decimals: `365.198.63.113` could be an IP address. Each computer or device connected to the Internet has a unique IP address. Some computers, usually servers, have fixed IP addresses. Other computers are issued dynamic addresses.

DNS

Numeric IP addresses are difficult to remember and easy to type incorrectly. In addition, they frequently change, either because they are dynamic or because the machine or device is moved to a new Internet host. Therefore, most practical Internet addressing uses domain names, such as `www.quepublishing.com`, rather than IP addresses.

Addressing through domain names relies on the Domain Name Service, or DNS, which maps domain names to IP addresses.

The World Wide Web

The World Wide Web is an application running on top of the Internet. The Web can be thought of as a vast network of documents that are transmitted on request over the Internet through the Hypertext Transfer Protocol (HTTP). HTTP can be used to transport many kinds of files, but the Web is generally thought of and used as a collection of static and dynamic HTML (Hypertext Markup Language) pages.

Static Web pages consist of fixed content and HTML markup code, which is used by browsers to display a structured and formatted document.

Dynamic Web pages contain server-side processing code, sometimes in combination with static HTML content. The server-side code is processed by an application server, which generates content and HTML markup dynamically, and then delivers an HTML page to a Web server that, in turn, returns it to a Web browser.

CAUTION

Server-side processing requires specific applications, such as CGI scripts, or application servers, such as ColdFusion. You cannot simply invoke server-side processing by creating a page with a .cfm or .asp extension.

Pages are grouped into Web sites. Sites are associated pages created by a person or an organization; they consist of a collection of related pages along with dependent files such as images, style sheets, video clips, and so forth.

Much of the power of the Web derives from the fact that Web pages can be linked electronically so that users can click hyperlinks (sometimes called *hotspots*) in one document to request another document. Links can be made between pages on a site to allow users to browse the entire site without manually entering a request for a specific page. Links can also be made between pages on different sites so that users can traverse documents located all over the world simply by clicking hyperlinks.

Web Browsers

Web browsers are desktop applications, also called client applications, used to request and process Web pages. Browsers parse HTML code and use the markup tags to render Web pages as rich text with embedded images and other media.

Current browsers do a great deal more than parse and render HTML. They can also display graphics in formats such as GIF, JPEG, and PNG, process Cascading Style Sheets (CSS) to derive sophisticated rules for displaying content, and interpret JavaScript to provide generation and manipulation of content through client-side scripting. Browsers can also work with plug-in applications to display other kinds of content, such as PDF files and Flash movies.

During the past five years, the browser market has been almost totally dominated by Netscape Navigator and Microsoft's Internet Explorer. Internet Explorer currently dominates the market; about 90% of users are estimated to use Internet Explorer as a primary Web browser.

Cross-Browser Compatibility

Internet Explorer and Netscape differ in their support of HTML, JavaScript, and CSS; therefore, the same page will be rendered somewhat differently in the two browsers. A larger problem is that JavaScript that works in one browser may produce errors in the other, producing annoying or alarming error messages and sometimes making pages unusable.

To make matters worse, significant differences exist between various versions of the same browser because browser makers continually struggle to keep up with rapidly evolving Web technology standards. They sometimes deviate from those standards as well, introducing proprietary tags and scripting capabilities in an attempt to provide distinctive value to users and developers. Creating pages that work well across different browsers and browser versions has been one the greatest challenges for Web developers.

NOTE

Dreamweaver helps address cross-browser compatibility problems in several ways, which will be addressed in Chapters 6, "Using Layers for Page Layout," and 14, "Formatting with Cascading Style Sheets."

Web Servers

A Web server is an application that sends files over the Web in response to requests from browsers. Each Web page that is viewed in a browser generally requires several requests to the server: one for the page itself and additional requests for dependent files issued by the browser automatically as it parses the code on the page.

The Web Document Root

Requests to a Web server ask for specific files. The request `http://www.macromedia.com/support/index.htm`, for instance, asks for the file named index.htm in the directory support. But where is the directory called support?

For security reasons, Web servers cannot send just any file that exists on the server; you would not want any user on the Internet to be able to download Registry data for the system, for example. Access is restricted to files located somewhere in the directory tree under a specific directory designated by the Web server administrator as the Web document root, sometimes referred to as the Web root. In addition to directories physically located under the Web document root, the server administrator may create mappings to other "virtual" directories that may be located anywhere on the server or on a mapped network drive that is accessible to the server.

Generally, Web servers also have a list of default files that they search for when a request points to a directory rather than to a specific file. This list is also managed by the server administrator but typically includes filenames such as index.html, index.htm, default.htm, and so forth. When no default page is found, the server will return a listing of all files in the directory, unless directory browsing is denied. The majority of servers disallow directory browsing for security reasons.

TIP

The order of the search varies according to the way the list is set up, so developers who provide a default page in each directory, which is a good practice, need to find out what the default names and search order are from the server administrator or create multiple copies of the default page with several names.

Web Servers and Server-Side Processing

Web servers generally do not process pages but simply send them to browsers. Web servers may process pages or initiate some kind of associated processing on the server for the following special types of files:

- Server Side Includes (SSI)—SSI files, usually marked with the special file extension .shtml, are processed by the Web server before they are sent to the browser. Special SSI tags are processed to insert dynamic information, such as the date, or to launch external processes such as database queries to generate dynamic content.
- Common Gateway Interface (CGI) applications—CGI applications reside in a special directory under the Web document root (/cgi-bin) and are invoked by browser requests. CGI programs can perform processing of various kinds and return content in a generated Web page.
- Web application servers—Requested files with special extensions are passed to an application server such as ColdFusion. The application server processes any server-side processing code in the page and uses it to generate content returned to the Web server, which in turn sends it to the browser.

URLs

A request from a Web browser that allows it to communicate with a Web server and retrieve documents is made in the form of a Uniform Resource Locator, or URL.

A URL may consist of a service identifier, hostname (IP address or DNS name), a path, and filename.

Following is a simple URL with an explanation of its parts:

http://www.w3.org/MarkUp/Guide/Advanced.html

Service identifier:	http:
Internet address:	//www.w3.org
Path:	/MarkUp/Guide/
File:	Advanced.html

The domain name directs the request to the appropriate server. The path is used by the Web server to locate the directory in the directory tree under the Web document root. The filename is used to identify the specific file requested. As you have already seen, if no filename is specified, the Web server will search for a default document.

A URL may include the following information as well:

- A specific port number used by the Web server instead of the default port for HTTP. The port number is appended to the domain name, separated from it by a colon (`:`). (A port is a specific area of memory on the system reserved for data involved in certain kinds of network communications.)
- A named anchor in an HTML page, appended to the filename and separated from it by a pound sign (`#`).
- A query string consisting of one or more `name=value` pairs, separated by ampersands (`&`). The entire query string is appended to the end of the URL, separated by a question mark (`?`).

Following is an example of a URL containing a port number, a named anchor, and a query string:

```
http://www.shophere.com:1234/products/bikes.html#racing?id=s086&name=Robert
```

Client-Side Web Technologies

Dreamweaver's greatest strength is in allowing you to exploit the primary client-side Web technologies—HTML, CSS, and JavaScript—in a visual, word processing-like mode, without having to spend a lot of time typing code manually. To get the most out of Dreamweaver, though, it is important to understand the technologies that the visual editor works with.

In this section, we look at the basics of the major client-side technologies for the Web: HTML, CSS, JavaScript, DHTML, and plug-in technologies.

NOTE

Other scripting languages, notably VBScript, can be used in Web pages. The broad browser support for JavaScript has made it by far the most commonly used language, and this book will not discuss other languages.

HTML

HTML provides a set of tags that can be inserted into a text file to indicate the logical structure of a document:

Sample: HTML Code

```
<h1>This is a level 1 heading</h1>
<h2>Level 2 heading</h2>
<p>Paragraph</p>
<ul>
  <li>Unordered list item</li>
  <li>another unordered list item</li>
</ul>
<table>
  <tr>
    <td>Table data cell</td>
    <td>Another table cell</td>
  </tr>
</table>
<pre>Preformatted text</pre>
```

In addition to describing the structure of the document, tags serve several other functions, such as

- Creating hyperlinks to other documents
- Embedding images and other media objects
- Linking the document to a style sheet
- Providing metainformation about the document
- Embedding JavaScript or CSS code

HTML Syntax

All HTML tags have the same basic syntax:

Sample: HTML Syntax

```
<tagname attribute1="value" attribute2="value"...>
        Textual content
</tagname>
```

All tags that contain textual content require closing tags: `<em>Emphasized text</em>`. Empty tags (those that contain no content, such as the `<br>` and `<img>` tags) must also be closed under the XHTML specification by including a forward slash at the end of the tag: `<img src="image1.gif" / >`.

> **NOTE**
>
> XHTML is a version of HTML refined to adhere to the requirements of XML languages. XHTML is the current recommended specification for HTML, although very few Web sites currently conform completely to the XHTML specification.

Many tags can take attributes, and some attributes, such as the `src` attribute for the `<img>` tag, are required. All attribute values should be enclosed in quotation marks.

> **NOTE**
>
> HTML is not case sensitive. XHTML is, however, and compliance with the XHTML specification requires that all tag and attribute names be lowercase.

Global Structure of HTML Documents

The overall structure of an HTML document contains the following parts.

HTML Version Information

The `<!DOCTYPE>` tag (an SGML, not HTML, tag) at the beginning of the document identifies the HTML DTD to which the document conforms.

The HTML Element

The `<html>` tag serves as a wrapper for the document. The entire document is enclosed between `<html>` and `</html>` tags.

The Document Head

The document head contains global information about the document. Some of that information is used by a browser in processing the document itself. Other information is primarily used by indexing services and search engines. The elements that make up the head section of the document are listed in Table 1.1.

Table 1.1 The Elements That Make Up the Document Head

Element	Description
The `<HEAD>` element	The `<head>` tag is a wrapper for all elements within the document head.
The `<TITLE>` element	The `<title>` tag encloses a title that typically appears in the title bar of the browser and is used as a primary identifier by many search engines.
Metadata	Metadata, contained in the attributes of one or more `<meta>` tags, provides information such as a summary of the page's contents and keywords, used primarily by indexing services and search engines.

Table 1.1 continued

Element	Description
Linked and embedded style sheets and scripts	The `<link>` tag is used in the document head most often to define a link to an external style sheet for the page. A style sheet can also be embedded in the document head using the `<style>` tag.

Depending on how it is used, a `<script>` tag may embed JavaScript code or provide a link (via the `src` attribute) to an external JavaScript file.

The Document Body

The document body contains all content meant to be rendered in the browser window and all tags that are used to structure the page content. The body can contain many other tags that can be divided into a few main groups, which are listed in Table 1.2.

Table 1.2 The Primary Elements of the Body

Element	Description
The `<BODY>` element	The `<body>` tag serves as a wrapper for content. Attributes of the tag can be used to define overall page features, such as background and text color.
Grouping elements: The `<DIV>` and `<SPAN>` elements	The most basic content-structuring elements are the `<div>` and `<span>` tags, which serve to group blocks and inline strings of content, respectively. These tags generally are used with CSS for page layout or to apply a style rule to a string within a block.
Headings: the `<H1>`, `<H2>`, `<H3>`, `<H4>`, `<H5>`, `<H6>` elements	The Hx headings provide the primary structuring of page content by indicating the hierarchical relationships between blocks of content.
Block-level and inline elements	Block-level elements distinguish different kinds of content blocks, such as paragraphs, lists, and tables. Inline elements set off strings within blocks, such as emphasized text, citations, and code.

> **NOTE**
>
> Coverage of individual tags and attributes is beyond the scope of this book. Consult the HTML reference that is included with Dreamweaver 4.

Structure and Display Specifications

Although the HTML specifications maintained by the World Wide Web Consortium (W3C) offer guidelines on how marked-up content blocks should be rendered, in principle it is up to the browser (or other application) to decide how to display the contents. The important thing is not what font and size are use to display different heading levels, but that a user is able to visually distinguish one level from another.

In practice, HTML tags are often used to specify formatting or display specifications, as well as structure. HTML acquired new tags (such as `<center>` and `<font>`) and attributes (such as `align` and `hspace`) aimed at giving developers more control over the appearance of rendered HTML in the mid-1990s, before Cascading Style Sheets were introduced.

Cascading Style Sheets are now well supported by almost all browsers in use, however, and much can be gained by separating the structure of content from its display specification. For this reason, the HTML 4.0 specification and the XHTML 1.0 stipulate using HTML for structuring only and specifying all formatting through style sheets. All tags and attributes whose sole purpose is to define formatting have been deprecated, meaning that their use is not recommended and they are likely to become obsolete in future specifications.

HTML Specifications

HTML specifications are maintained by the W3C. The latest—and final—HTML specification is 4.1. The HTML specifications are now considered superceded by the XHTML specifications (the current XHTML specification is 1.0, and a 1.1 specification also exists for modularized XHTML).

CSS

Cascading Style Sheets enable you to specify display characteristics for documents structured with HTML or XML tags. Style sheets can written in external files linked to one or more pages or embedded in individual pages using the `<style>` tag. Inline CSS styles can also be applied through the `style` attribute, but the style attribute is deprecated in the XHTML specifications because it violates the principle of separating content structure from formatting.

CSS Syntax

CSS rules consist of a selector, which specifies what element the rule is applied to, and `property:value` pairs for the rule enclosed in braces and separated by semicolons:

Sample: CSS Rules

```
selector {property1 : value; property2 : value ...}
```

The following are five types of selectors:

- Tag—Any tag name or a comma-delimited list of tag names
- Class—A class name attached to a tag in the document through the class attribute
- ID—A unique tag ID in the page, specified in the tag through the id attribute
- Pseudoclass—A special instance of content, such as a hyperlink in a particular state or the first letter of a paragraph
- Contextual—A tag, only when it occurs in the context of another specific tag

The following code sample gives an example of each style rule using each of the selector types listed previously:

Sample: CSS Code Illustrating the Different Selector Types

```
p (font-family: sans-serif; font-size: 12px}
.highlight {background-color: #FFFF00}
#logo {text-align: center; font-weight: bold}
a:hover {color: red}
p em {font-style: italic}
```

CSS is not case sensitive. Style sheets for XHTML documents should use lowercase for tag selectors, however.

Cascading Order

Because a linked style sheet and an embedded style sheet (and under the HTML specification, inline styles) can be applied to the same page, it is possible to create multiple style rules for the same selector. The cascading order resolves conflicting values for the same style properties by giving precedence to the style definition closest to the element. In other words, inline styles take precedence over embedded styles, and embedded styles take precedence over linked styles. All nonconflicting properties are applied to the element.

Inheritance

Some, but not all, style properties are inherited. A `<strong>` tag nested inside a <p> tag, for instance, would inherit properties such as the font-family defined for paragraphs, but would not inherit border or padding properties. In case of conflicting values for the same property, values for the element's own style rule take precedence over inherited values.

CSS Specifications

Two CSS specifications are maintained by the W3C: CSS1 and CSS2. CSS1 is largely supported by Internet Explorer, Netscape 4+, and Opera 3.5+. Support for CSS2 is limited; Internet Explorer, Netscape, and Opera all support CSS2 positioning, however.

> **NOTE**
>
> A complete description of CSS properties is beyond the scope of this book. A complete CSS reference is included in Dreamweaver.

JavaScript

JavaScript is an object-based scripting language designed for use on the Web, although it has been used for other purposes, such as creating extensions for Dreamweaver. JavaScript has evolved considerably since it was first introduced and is implemented somewhat differently in different browsers, making cross-browser compatibility a challenge for Web developers.

JavaScript consists of a set of commands, control structures, functions, and built-in objects.

> **NOTE**
> JavaScript should not be confused with the Java programming language. Although some similarity in syntax exists between the two languages, there is no direct connection between them.

Much of the value of JavaScript for use in HTML pages derives from its capability to access and manipulate the following data objects, which are generated by the browser in client memory:

- Navigator objects—Objects that contain the properties of the browser itself; the navigator objects allow the script to assess the browser's capabilities.
- Window objects—Objects that contain the properties of the browser window; methods such as `open()` and `close()` also allow scripts to manipulate browser windows.
- Document Object Model (DOM)—A collection of objects associated with the elements that make up the page.

Some object properties can only be read by a script; others can be set to modify properties of the document. Many objects also have associated methods that allow the script to perform an action, such as displaying an alert in the window or writing code and content in the document.

Execution of object methods or JavaScript commands and functions can occur when the page loads or in response to events such as mouseover and mouseout. Event-based scripting uses the event attributes of HTML tags to tie objects on the page to events.

JavaScript Syntax

JavaScript is case sensitive, although the degree of sensitivity varies between Netscape's JavaScript and Microsoft's JScript implementations. Commands must be separated by a semicolon and/or a linebreak.

The example that follows shows a simple JavaScript function that takes two arguments, x and y, and writes the sum and product of the arguments into the document.

Sample: JavaScript Code

```
function sumAndProduct(x,y) {
    // sum
```

```
    document.write("Sum: " x+y)
    // product
    document.write("Product: "x*y)
}
```

DHTML

DHTML is not a distinct technology in the way that HTML, CSS, and JavaScript are. Rather, it is a term introduced by both Netscape and Microsoft to describe new capabilities of their 4.0 browsers. By DHTML, they mean the capability to manipulate an HTML page on the client system. In most cases, DHTML has been used to describe the manipulation of the appearance of page elements, covering such effects as dynamic pop-up or drop-down menus, animations, and cinematic features such as dissolving or fading of pages.

Beneath the descriptions, Netscape and Microsoft implemented DHTML in significantly different ways, the difficulty of creating cross-browser DHTML has limited its use considerably. With the help of some intervention by the W3C, the two major browser makers have moved closer together on DHTML, and in current browser versions, it is accurate to say that DHTML consists primarily of manipulation of style properties through JavaScript to modify page elements.

> **NOTE**
>
> Dreamweaver's powerful tools for generating DHTML effects are covered in Chapter 19, "Using Behaviors."

Summary

- The Internet is a global network of computers and devices that are identified by unique IP addresses.
- In practice, Internet addressing often uses domain names that are mapped to IP addresses.
- Data is transmitted over the Internet using the TCP/IP protocol.
- The World Wide Web runs on top of the Internet using the HTTP protocol.
- The World Wide Web consists of electronically linked HTML files and other files that can be displayed or downloaded by a Web browser.
- There are many Web browsers, each having somewhat different capabilities, but all share the main function of interpreting HTML code and rendering HTML documents.
- In addition to HTML code, Web documents may include code for style sheets or to invoke processing on the server or client.
- The most important client-side Web technologies, apart from HTML, are cascading style sheets and JavaScript.

Sample Questions

1. Which of the following is not a valid URL?
   - A. `http://127.0.0.1/index.htm`
   - B. `http://www.quest.com/products/widget.htm`
   - C. `http://www.quest.com/index.htm?id=001`
   - D. `http://topserver/index.htm&nav.htm`

2. Which of the following is not a standardized technology covered by a World Wide Web Consortium specification?
   - A. `XHTML`
   - B. `DHTML`
   - C. `CSS`
   - D. `XML`

CHAPTER 2

Using the Macromedia Dreamweaver Interface

Introduction

Macromedia Dreamweaver is a powerful site-development tool and therefore has a user interface with many components. In this chapter, we will look at the most important ones.

Document Window

The heart of Dreamweaver is the Document window, in which documents are edited. At the top of the window is a menu that provides access to most of Dreamweaver's functionality. Particularly relevant to editing Web documents are the Insert, Modify, and Text menus, which enable you to insert many kinds of elements into a page, to modify those elements (and properties of a page, as well), and to structure or format text via HTML tags and attributes or CSS styles. Many of these commands are included in the context-sensitive right-click (on Macintosh CTRL+click) menus available inside the editing space.

Beneath the menus is a toolbar that provides quick access to the following functions:

- Code view—(Discussed later in this chapter)
- Split view—(Discussed later in this chapter)
- Design view—The default view, for visual editing of pages
- Title field—For quick entry of document title
- File Management—For getting and putting files from and to the remote site, accessing design notes, and checking files in and out

- Preview/Debug in Browser—Preview or debug the current page in an external browser; manage the external browser list
- Refresh Design View—To refresh the Design view if changes that affect the rendering have been made to the document outside the Document window
- Reference—To access the HTML/CSS/JavaScript references
- Code Navigator—To set and remove breakpoints for JavaScript debugging
- View Options—To change view options (the submenu depends on which view is current)

The status bar at the bottom of the Document window contains several tools. On the left side is the Tag Selector (discussed in a later section). Next, toward the right, is the Window Size tool, which can be used to resize the Document window to see the pixel dimensions of the page contents.

> **NOTE**
>
> The Tag Selector is visible only when the cursor is in the Design view.

Next is the Document Weight/Download Time indicator, showing the total data weight of the page and its dependencies and the approximate download time. The connection speed used to calculate download time can be set in the Dreamweaver Preferences.

The Launcher on the right side of the status bar provides quick access to frequently used tool panels such as the Assets, CSS Styles, and Behaviors panels. You can specify which panels are shown in the Launcher in the Panels category of the Dreamweaver Preferences.

By default, the editing area of the Document window presents the Design view, where HTML and other Web documents (CFML, ASP, and so on) can be edited visually with the aid of the Property Inspector (discussed in a later section). Although not a Web browser, the Document window provides an approximate rendering of HTML tags. It also renders some, but not all, CSS styling. Various icons are used to indicate the position in the code of specially positioned or invisible elements, such as layers and line breaks.

Code and Split Views

In addition to the Design mode, Dreamweaver provides a Code view that enables you to edit HTML code directly. Although it's not as full-featured as code editors such as HomeSite, Code view supports color coding of tag syntax, autoindenting, line numbering, and word wrap. These options can be toggled on and off using the View, Code View Options menu. Color coding and code formatting can be configured in the Dreamweaver Preferences.

The Split view displays both the Design and Code views in a split window to give you access to both. You can click and drag the bar that splits the window to adjust the amount of space devoted to each view. Dragging the bar all the way to the top or bottom of the window switches you to full Design or Code view, respectively. (When you return to the Split view, the previous position of the splitter bar will be restored.)

> **TIP**
>
> The easiest way to examine or edit the code behind a page element is to select it in the Design view (by clicking and dragging over the element or using the Tag Selector); then switch to the Code or Split view, where the corresponding code will also be selected.

Tag Selector

The Tag Selector, located in the lower-left corner of the Document window on the status bar, is a useful tool for ensuring that you are modifying the correct tag. Wherever the cursor or selection is located in the Document window, the Tag Selector shows the current tag stack for that content, which means that the outermost tag in a nested set (generally the `<body>` tag) is shown on the left, and progressively nested tags are shown in order from left to right. The tag shown at the right end of the stack is the closest to the cursor or selection.

> **NOTE**
>
> The Tag Selector is visible only when the cursor is in the Design view.

To select a tag and all its contents, position the cursor so that the tag shows up in the Tag Selector and then click the tag in the Selector to select it. The technique is especially effective for selecting a table row or a nested table or when you want to move content and ensure that its tag wrapper stays with the content.

The Tag Selector has other useful functions that you can access by right-clicking a tag to open a drop-down menu. This menu enables you to do the following:

- Remove the tag, leaving its contents intact.
- Open a code-based Quick Tag Editor to manually edit the HTML code for the tag; the Quick Tag Editor is context sensitive and will display a drop-down list of available attributes you can select when you insert a space after the tag name or an existing attribute.
- Set the CSS class for the tag from a list of classes defined in linked or embedded style sheets for the page. (You can also remove an existing class by setting the class to `none`.)
- Set the ID for the tag from a list of IDs defined in linked or embedded style sheets for the page. (You can also remove an existing ID by setting the class to `none`.)

Tool Panels

Many of Dreamweaver's powerful editing tools can be accessed through one of several tool panels. These panels can all be toggled open and closed using the Document window Window menu. The Launcher on the Document window status bar (described earlier) also allows you to toggle the view of the selected panels on and off. Each panel also has a small "x" in the upper-left or upper-right corner that you can click to close the panel.

To maximize the use of screen space, most tool windows contain multiple tabbed panels. You can click and drag a section by its tab to put it in a window by itself or drop it into a different tool window.

The remainder of this section describes some of the most commonly used panels in more detail.

Property Inspector

The Property Inspector, which can be docked to the Document window by dragging it until it "clicks" into place, provides quick access to the most commonly used content-formatting features. The Inspector is context-sensitive, displaying formatting options for the current selection or for the innermost tag in the current tag stack if no content is selected.

> **TIP**
>
> You can use the Tag Selector or, in some cases, special icons or handles in the Document window to select specific tags and gain access to their associated properties.

The Property Inspector, by default, shows basic formatting options for the current context. For many contexts (a table cell, for instance), you can display advanced formatting options by clicking the small toggle icon that is located at the lower-right corner of the Inspector window.

Although the Property Inspector is context-sensitive, the options it offers do not all apply directly to the immediate or nearest tag. Some options do add or modify tag attributes, but others, such as font face, size, and color selectors, result in the insertion of a new tag (in this case the `<font>` tag). For layers implemented through `<div>` tags, several of the options generate CSS properties that are assigned to the `<div>` tag via the style attribute.

You can view context-sensitive help by clicking the "?" icon on the right side of the Property Inspector. Below the Help icon is another icon that invokes the Quick Tag Editor (described earlier in this chapter).

Objects Panel

The Objects panel allows you to insert a wide range of simple and complex elements into your page (these elements can also be inserted using the Insert menu in the Document window). Some objects are inserted into the page at the current cursor location when you click an icon on the Objects panel. Other objects take parameters that you specify in a dialog box that opens when you click the icon to insert the object.

The Objects panel contains several categories of objects, accessible through the categories chooser button at the top of the panel:

- Common—Includes commonly used HTML objects, such as images, tables, horizontal rules, and layers, as well as more rollover images and server-side includes; the Common objects also provide a point of integration with other Macromedia tools, allowing you to insert Fireworks HTML, Flash .swf files, Flash text and buttons, and more.
- Characters—Includes icons for the most commonly used special character codes such as the nonbreaking space and copyright symbol, as well as a general selector for special characters; although technically not a character, the line break `<br>` can also be inserted from the Characters objects.
- Forms—Enables you to insert forms and form controls.
- Frames—Enables you to insert eight different framesets that span the most commonly used frame configurations.
- Head—Enables you to insert elements that belong in the document head section, such as meta tags and link tags.
- Invisibles—Enables you to insert elements that are not visible in the rendered page: named anchors, comments, and scripts (the location of these elements is marked by icons in the Document window that correspond to the Objects panel icons).
- Special—Enables insertion of non-HTML elements such as Java applets, ActiveX controls, and other objects requiring browser plug-ins for processing.

In addition to the different object categories, four icons used for designing pages using HTML tables are located at the bottom of the Objects panel. These icons allow you to toggle between Normal and Layout mode and to draw layout tables or insert new layout table cells. Layout tables are discussed in Chapter 7, "Using Tables for Page Layout."

Extending the Objects panel with new categories and objects is covered in Chapter 16, "Libraries and Extensions."

Assets Panel

The Assets panel serves as a tool for organizing and inserting media assets for the site. The Assets panel automatically scans the site directories for media assets when you create or modify a site and creates media catalogs for you, dividing assets into types discussed later in this section. For all assets except Templates and Library Items, the Assets panel offers two views of your assets:

- Site—An alphabetical list of all assets (of a type) for the site
- Favorites—Favorite assets, which can be arranged into virtual folders

> **TIP**
>
> Site assets are especially useful for sites with a small number of images or other media files that are spread over several folders. Having them all in a single list cuts down the time spent searching for the image you want.

> **CAUTION**
> If you add or delete media assets after setting up the site, do so from the Site window so that the Assets panel will register the changes.

Organizing your assets into Favorites, creating a virtual folder for each page or section of the site, will speed up page development and decrease the likelihood of using the wrong asset files.

Asset Categories

Assets are divided into nine categories, which can be viewed by clicking the category icons that appear along the left side of the Assets panel:

- Images—All JPEG, GIF, and PNG image files in the site
- Colors—All colors used in the site pages
- URLs—External URLs used in links
- Flash—Flash files in the site folders
- Shockwave—Shockwave files in the site folders
- Movies—Movie files in the site folders
- Scripts—Script files in the site folders
- Templates—Dreamweaver template files (.dwt) in the site folders
- Library Items—Library items defined for the site

Reference Panel

The Reference panel contains references for HTML, CSS, and JavaScript. You can access these references directly, or from Code view, you can right-click menus for reference entries on specific elements.

Site Window

Although you can use Dreamweaver as a simple document editor, defining sites enables you to take advantage of the site management tools, which include the following:

- Automatic updating of links, templates, and library items
- Link checking
- Report generation on missing ALT attributes, empty tags, nested `<font>` tags that could be combined, and so on
- Sitewide check for compatibility with target browsers
- Synchronization of local and remote sites
- Design notes

Sites are managed through the Site window, which opens automatically when you define or open a site. Site definitions are created by selecting Site, New Site, and can be reopened for modification later.

The Site window enables you to view your site structure in several ways. There are two panes: the right pane shows the folder/file structure of the local site; the left pane shows the remote site (if defined) or the site map (if a home page is defined). The left pane can be toggled in and out of view by clicking the icon that appears in the lower-left corner of the Site window.

File-management operations, such as creating and moving folders and files, can be carried out from the Site window. In addition, the various testing and deployment tools can be accessed here. These tools can be accessed from the Document window as well, but some (such as Check Target Browsers) must be accessed through the Site window to perform the action on the entire site.

The Site window is also useful in conjunction with the Point to File tool in the Property Inspector, which can be dragged over files in the Site window to create hyperlinks to pages within the site or to define source files for images.

The Site Map

After specifying a home page in the Site Map Layout section of the site definition, you can view a site map in the left pane of the Site window. The site map shows links between the files, allowing you to view your site as a structure collection of pages rather than as grouped files. Any page can be set as the home page in the site map to give you a view of the navigation of the site from that starting point.

Customizing Dreamweaver

Dreamweaver can be customized and extended in many ways. Extensions are covered in a later chapter. Here we will look at the options exposed in the Preferences and Keyboard Shortcuts dialog boxes. Customization of the Site window is covered in a later section of this chapter.

Preferences

The Preferences dialog box, opened by selecting Edit, Preferences (or by pressing CTRL+U), offers such a wide range of customization options that even experienced users often overlook some useful ones. Preferences are grouped into 16 categories. The options in the different categories are covered in the following subsections.

General

In the General Preferences, you can select the following options:

- Display only the Site window when Dreamweaver is launched.
- Open a new blank page when Dreamweaver is launched.
- Provide a warning when read-only files are opened.
- Automatically add a specified extension to new files when they are saved (if none is provided by the user).
- Specify how Dreamweaver should handle the updating of links when a file is moved within the site.
- Specify whether a dialog box should be shown to modify default parameter values when an object is inserted.

- Defer some automatic updating of table properties to improve typing speed in Design view.
- Automatically rename pasted form items to avoid duplication of form control names.
- Enable double-byte input in the Document window (requires a development environment or language kit that supports double-byte characters).
- Set the maximum number of steps recorded in the history panel. (Oldest steps are discarded when the maximum is reached.)
- Specify the way that Objects panel items are displayed.
- Choose among available dictionaries for spell checking.

Color Coding

In the Color Coding Preferences, you can specify how tags are color coded in the Code view. You can specify general color settings and also overrides for specific tags.

Code Format

In the Code Format Preferences, you can choose the way that generated code is formatted in fine detail:

- Indenting—Specify whether to indent code, use spaces or tabs for indenting, and apply indenting to table and frames code; specify the number of spaces or size of tabs to use.
- Line Wrapping and Breaks—Specify whether to automatically wrap lines of code and at what point; specify which control characters to use to indicate line breaks (Windows, Macintosh, or Unix).
- Tag Case—Choose the case for tags and attributes, and specify whether Dreamweaver should enforce case rules in preexisting HTML files.
- Centering—Choose whether to use the `<center>` or `<div align="center">` tag for centering content.

TIP

HTML is not case sensitive, but XHTML is. Using lowercase for tags and attributes does no harm and helps to ensure XHTML compatibility for the future.

CAUTION

Dreamweaver correctly points out that the `<center>` tag is included in the HTML 4.0 transitional specification and is supported by a wider range of browsers than `<div align="center">`. However, the `<center>` tag is deprecated in the HTML 4.0 specification. It is worth noting that the align attribute is also deprecated in the XHTML specification because, like the `<center>` tag, its use is purely for display specification. The preferred alternative is to use style sheets for all display specification.

Code Rewriting

Dreamweaver can automatically repair many code errors, such as improperly nested tags or missing end tags. You can specify whether such errors should be automatically fixed and whether Dreamweaver should provide a warning before modifying any existing code.

You can also ask Dreamweaver to automatically replace spaces in URLs and special characters used in attribute values, because these might not be interpreted correctly in some browsers.

You can also choose to not let Dreamweaver clean up code in pages with specified extensions. This option is generally used to protect server-side scripting code, such as CFML intermixed with HTML code, from being misinterpreted as HTML syntax errors.

Dreamweaver 4 is very good at recognizing most server-side code for what it is, and it is not prone to misinterpreting it. The following line of code, for instance, will not be modified by either automatic or manually executed code cleanup:

```
<tr <cfif (q_order_detail.currentrow MOD 2 EQ 0)>bgcolor="yellow"</cfif>">
```

However, it is difficult to guarantee that some particularly complex combination of HTML code and server-side code would not be incorrectly "cleaned up." If you allow Dreamweaver to automatically clean up application pages, you should also enable the warning that code is going to be cleaned up so that you can decide whether to continue the clean-up operation.

CAUTION

Note also that even though Dreamweaver correctly recognizes server-side code, it does not interpret it; therefore, it may clean up HTML code in a way that conflicts with code generated by server-side scripting. For instance, look at the following code sample, in which the closing tag for the table was inserted by Dreamweaver to replace the one that is commented out:

```
<table cellspacing="5">
<cfoutput query="q_Order_Detail">
<tr <cfif (q_order_detail.currentrow MOD 2 EQ 0)>bgcolor="yellow"</cfif>">
<td>#q_Order_Detail.Line_No#</td>
     <td>#q_Order_Detail.Bean_Name#</td>
     <td align="right">#q_Order_Detail.Quantity#</td>
     <td align="right">#DollarFormat(q_Order_Detail.Price_Per_Unit)#</td>
     <td align="right">#q_Order_Detail.Discount_Percent#%</td>
</tr>
</cfoutput>
<!--</table> -->

<cfinclude template="/Included_Templates_Solution/footer.cfm">
</table>
```

CSS Styles

This category enables you to specify whether Dreamweaver should use an optional shorthand style for some complex style properties, such as those for fonts and borders. The only issues are the conciseness of the code in the style sheet and whether your target browsers support the shorthand form of the property definitions.

> **TIP**
>
> When in doubt, use the full form of the property definitions rather than the shorthand style; the full form has wider browser support. The amount of additional code in the style sheet will be trivial from a page-weight perspective.

File Types/Editors

This category covers options related to code editing, allowing you to define an external code editor and how Dreamweaver should respond when an open file is modified in an external editor. You can also specify extensions for files that should be opened in Code view and external applications for various media types.

Fonts/Encoding

This category allows you to set encoding and various font options for the Dreamweaver code view. These settings do not affect the way the document is rendered in a browser.

Highlighting

This category allows you toggle on and off and set colors for highlighting Editable Regions, Locked Regions, Library Items, and Third-Party Tags in the Design view.

Invisible Elements

This category allows you to choose which invisible elements (such as `<br>` tags) are indicated by an icon in the Design view.

Layers

The Layers category lets you choose the tag used to define layers and to set some default CSS properties for layers.

> **TIP**
>
> Use the `<div>` tag to define layers. The `<layer>` tag was introduced by Netscape 4.0 and is supported only by 4.x versions of Netscape.

Layout View

In Layout view, you can specify how Dreamweaver behaves when you create layout tables. The settings include whether spacer images should be inserted to manage spacing in autostretch tables and colors that should be used to indicate design elements in the Design view.

Panels

The Panels category enables you to specify which panels should always remain on top of the Document and Site windows, and which panels should appear in the Launcher.

Preview in Browser

This category enables you to add installed browsers to the list you can choose from to preview documents. You also can specify which of the browsers should be the primary one for previewing.

You can check an option to serve files through your local Web server when you browse them, so that server-side includes and other server-side processing can be previewed.

Quick Tag Editor

The Quick Tag Editor options include whether changes should be applied immediately and whether Dreamweaver should offer tag hints, which display drop-down lists of tags and attributes that can be selected to save typing.

Site

The site category contains preferences related to sites and the Site window. The options include the following:

- Which pane of the Site window in which to display local and remote files
- Whether Dreamweaver should prompt you to include dependent files during FTP transfers and check in/check out operations
- Whether to automatically disconnect FTP connections after specified idle time
- How long to attempt FTP connections before timing out
- Specify firewall settings
- Whether to save files automatically before putting

In addition to the settings available in Preferences, in the Site Definition dialog box in the Site window, you can set which file information columns to include, or you can select View, File View Columns. (This menu option is available only in the Site window.)

Status Bar

In this category you can set options for the Document window status bar. Window sizes can be added or modified for the Window Size menu. The connection speed can be specified for calculating the estimated download time for the page. Finally, you can choose whether the Launcher for panels should be displayed.

Creating and Naming Files

Several options exist for creating new files in Dreamweaver. One is to select File, New from the Document or File, New Window from the Site window to open a new document with the default template. The default template is called default.html and is located under the Dreamweaver 4 program directory, under \Configuration\Templates. This file can be edited or replaced to substitute a new default template.

The New from Template command, also under the File menu, enables you to create a new page using an existing Dreamweaver template. The dialog box allows you to choose templates defined for any site, although it normally makes sense to keep all templates used in a site within some directory in that site.

In the Site window only, you can select a folder and then select File, New File to create a new file in that folder. Also in the Site window, in the Site Map, you can right-click a file and select Link to New File to create both the link and the new file.

Summary

The Dreamweaver interface consists of three main components: the Document window, the Site window, and the tool panels. Pages can be edited in Design, Code, or Split view. Most functionality is available in multiple ways—through the menus, tool panels, the Document window toolbar, and the right-click menus for elements in pages or files and folders in the Site window. The Preferences dialog box enables you to change many options for both the Document and Site windows, as well as the way Dreamweaver responds to actions, such as modifying a file in an external editor.

Sample Questions

1. Which of the following is not included in the Assets panel?
   A. Style sheets
   B. Flash files
   C. Shockwave files
   D. Library items

2. Which of the following editing modes provides Tag Hints?
   A. Design view
   B. Code view
   C. Quick Tag Editor
   D. Code Inspector

CHAPTER 3

Creating a Local Site

Web Site Defined

Macromedia Dreamweaver enables you to develop and deploy your Web sites according to development best practices. As with any programming paradigm, it is recommended that you develop files separate from what a user can access. This enables developers to make changes to a site without any downtime and allows full testing prior to deploying new files.

Best practices suggest that you create your Web pages using the following three environments:

- A development server on which only Web site developers have access to the pages. These pages often are works in progress.
- A staging or test server on which members of a Quality Assurance team can test the pages with the assurance that they will not change in the middle of a test.
- A production server on which users are able to browse the end result Web site.

Local Site

In Dreamweaver, the term *site* can refer either to a Web site or to a local storage location for the documents belonging to a Web site. To create pages in a development environment, you are encouraged to create a local site. A *local site* in Dreamweaver is simply a folder on your hard drive under which your development work for a Web site will take place. This top-level directory is also known as a *root directory* of your Web site.

Folder Organization

When planning your Web site, take the time to plan your folder hierarchy. Some subfolders you may want to define under your root folder include the following:

- A folder, perhaps for each section of your Web site, as defined by your main navigation bar.
- An /images folder to contain images for the entire site or one /images folder under each section folder.
- Folders for other types of asset files, such as Flash movies, sounds, or videos.

You can create this folder hierarchy outside of Dreamweaver and set it as your local site, or you can define a local site and use Dreamweaver to create the subfolders for you.

Local Site Benefits

Dreamweaver enables you to create individual Web pages; however, many benefits exist to grouping these pages into a local site. Benefits include the following:

- The capability to update links to a page automatically when you move it within the site structure.
- All folders and files under the local site are displayed using the Site window. The Site window enables you to create, maintain, and deploy your Web site.
- When files are ready for testing or deployment into production, you can do so using FTP.
- Modifications to files can be uploaded to the production server because it keeps track of which files have changed and need to be redeployed.
- Files maintained within a local site can be collaboratively shared among developers.

Creating a Local Site

To create a local site within Dreamweaver, use the New Site command under the Site menu. Properties for a local site definition are shown in Table 3.1:

Table 3.1 Settings of a Local Site

Setting	Description
Site Name	This attribute should be set to a unique value that is meaningful to your Web site. It does not appear in the browser and is used only for your reference.
Local Root Folder	Specify the folder on your hard disk in which site files, templates, and library items will be stored. If the local root folder does not yet exist, you can create it using the file-browsing dialog box.

Table 3.1 continued

Setting	Description
Refresh Local File List Automatically	This option indicates whether to automatically refresh the local file list every time you copy files into your local site. Deselecting this option results in better performance when files are added. However, you will then have to manually refresh the Site window.
HTTP Address	This attribute value contains the URL that your completed Web site will use so that Dreamweaver can verify links within the site that use absolute URLs.
Cache	Indicate whether to create a local cache to improve the speed of link- and site-management tasks. If you do not select this option, Dreamweaver will ask you if you want to create a cache again before it creates the site. It is a good idea to select this option because the Assets panel works only if a cache is created.

TIP

Root-relative links are links to files and resources that are relative to the root directory of your Web site. If you use root-relative links in your documents, Dreamweaver will use the Local Root Folder setting to do so.

→ Refer to Chapter 15, "Site Assets" for more information on the Assets panel.

Site Window

After you create a local site, the Site window displays. This interface enables you to manage all site files. You can move, rename, delete, copy, paste, and open files within this interface. Local site files and folders are displayed on the right side of this window.

You can also specify a remote site. A remote site is the intended production server and file path used for a working Web site. If you have created a remote site, the remote files are shown on the left pane of this window.

Preferences

You can alter the appearance and settings for the local site using the Dreamweaver Preferences dialog box and choosing the Site category. Choose Edit, Preferences to open the dialog. Site settings that you can alter are shown in Table 3.2:

Table 3.2 Attributes of a Remote Site

Setting	Description
Always Show [Local/Remote] on the [Left/Right]	This setting enables you to reverse the left-to-right order of the local and remote panes on the Site window.
Dependent Files	This setting enables the display of a prompt for transferring dependent files (such as images) that the browser loads when it loads the HTML file.
FTP Settings	These settings determine whether the connection to the remote site is terminated after the specified numbers of minutes have passed with no activity. If there is no response after the specified amount of time, Dreamweaver displays a warning dialog box alerting the user.
Firewall Settings	These settings enable you to set the address of the proxy server and the port, if it is other than the standard 21.
Put Options: Save Files Before Putting	This option indicates that unsaved files are saved automatically before being put onto the remote site.
Define Sites	This button brings up the Define Sites dialog box, in which you can edit an existing site or create a new one.

→ Refer to Chapter 20, "Team Collaboration," for more information on file check in/out.

Remote Site

After you have created a local site, you can then associate a remote site for deployment. A remote site can either be on a server that is on the local network (using a mapped drive) or on another server on the Internet (using FTP).

Your local site and your remote site should have the same folder hierarchy. If you use Dreamweaver to create the site and then deploy it to the remote site, Dreamweaver ensures that the local structure is duplicated on the remote site.

Use the Site, Define Sites dialog box to choose the local site to edit. When you receive the Site Definition dialog box, choose the Remote Info category.

Local/Network

Use the Local/Network Server Access option if your Web server is mounted as a network drive (Windows), an AppleTalk or NFS server (Macintosh), or if the Web server is running on your local machine in a separate directory from the local site.

Properties for setting up a local/network remote server are shown in Table 3.3.

Table 3.3 Attributes of a Local/Network Remote Site

Attribute	Description
Remote Folder	Use the Browse button to find the folder on the remote machine for deployment.
Refresh Remote File List Automatically	Update the remote file list automatically as files are added and deleted. For increased speed when copying files to the remote site, leave this option unselected. Manually refresh the Site window at any time using the Site window's Refresh button.
Check In/Out Settings	These settings enable Dreamweaver to enable check in/out and automatically check out a file when you open it. Specifying your name in the Check Out Name attribute enables other team members to view who is working on the file.
E-mail Address	For sites designated as check in/out, input your e-mail address so that team members can e-mail you questions about files that you have checked out.

FTP

By selecting FTP as your remote server access method, you are prompted for all the information necessary to connect to the FTP site. FTP settings are discussed next in Table 3.4:

Table 3.4 Attributes of an FTP Remote Site

Setting	Description
FTP Host	Enter the hostname of the FTP host using the format *ftp.domain.com*.
Host Directory	Name of the host directory at the remote site in which documents visible to the public are stored.

Table 3.4 continued

Setting	Description
Login/Password [Save]	FTP login information. You can uncheck the Save check box to tell Dreamweaver to prompt you for a password each time you connect to the remote server.
Firewall Settings	Check these settings if you are behind a firewall and if you want to use passive FTP, which lets your local software set up the FTP connection rather than requesting the remote server to do so.

CAUTION

Dreamweaver's FTP implementation is different from some common FTP applications. In particular, you must connect to the remote system's root folder, and you cannot navigate through the remote file system.

TIP

Slow connections may cause FTP timeouts to occur. Increasing the timeout value in Site Preferences may alleviate some problems.

WebDAV and SourceSafe Integration

Dreamweaver lets you access source- and version-control applications from the Site window. You can connect to SourceSafe databases and servers or source-control systems that support the WebDAV protocol.

After you are connected, you can use Dreamweaver's file-sharing features, such as Check In/Out, Refresh, Get and Put, and Design Notes to access corresponding features found in your own source-control system.

NOTE

To use this feature, you must have Visual SourceSafe installed on your system or have access to a system supported by WebDAV.

Summary

Creating a local site enables you to maintain all files and folders using the Site window. The Site window gives you the benefits of maintaining links within the site, as well as helps you to deploy your completed and maintained files into production. A remote site can be specified for a local site to deploy the files to either a LAN mapped drive or an FTP site.

Sample Questions

1. How can Dreamweaver deploy a local site to a remote site? Choose two.
   A. HTTP
   B. A mapped drive
   C. Telnet
   D. FTP

2. Which one is not a benefit of using the Site window?
   A. File edit rollbacks
   B. Automatic link updates
   C. Team collaboration
   D. FTP deployment

CHAPTER 4

Design Basics

Defining the Goal

Good Web-site design always begins with the same step—an understanding of the problem being solved. Without understanding the reason for the creation of the Web site itself, you will never be able to determine when you are done or how successful you have been. Putting the goal, or need, in an easy-to-understand format will also allow those around you to understand and, if needed, approve your development efforts.

The goal of your Web site will define your user base, which, in turn, will suggest which technology can or cannot be used. It will also suggest methods for organizing the information in your site and for building navigation around it.

After you understand these things, you can better use Macromedia Dreamweaver to design your site, build your site, and maintain your site. You will find that no matter what kind of site you are building, Dreamweaver has tools in it that will help you in all three of these phases.

To illustrate the importance of understanding the problem, let's look at three types of sites and the implications of their designs:

- Online catalog site—A client who sells blank computer media has asked your company to develop a Web site for them. The idea is to move its catalog online so that clients can browse its standard inventory and make buying decisions before contacting a salesperson. Later, the system may be adapted to accept orders online from established customers.
- Online training site—Your company manufactures synthetic bones used in reconstructive surgery and needs to

build and maintain an area on the company intranet where salespeople in the field can be trained on the newest products.
- Poetry corner—In an effort to make the world a better place, you have decided to start your own Web site where people can read your latest poetry creations or browse through old archives. The site will be a fun place for people with your interests to gather, read, and submit their own works.

You may find it helpful to go through a similar thought process with all your Web sites.

Define the Audience

People come to a Web site because they are looking for the Web site to do something for them. If you understand what problem your Web site is going to solve, you will have defined what people will be drawn to your site—those looking to solve that type of problem. Let's use the three examples from the previous section to further illustrate this point:

- Online catalog site—People most interested in browsing the online catalog of blank computer media will be current and potential customers of the client. Because they are from the computer industry, they will probably be fairly computer and Web savvy, have up-to-date hardware and software, and have at least a rough idea of what they are looking for.
- Online training site—Users of this site will be receiving training on the latest company products. Interested parties may be salespeople or clients, but because the training is to reside on the intranet, we know that only company employees, and mainly salespeople, will be accessing the site. All employees are trained on the basics of the company's products, and the salespeople are trained even more extensively. Because there is a policy regarding the standard computer platform, operating system, and browser software in the company, we know exactly which browser all our users will be using.
- Poetry corner—Users of this site will have an interest in reading or discussing poetry. Potentially, our user could be using any platform, any browser, and any version. But statistically, our user is likely to match the profile of a typical Internet user. This allows us to make educated guesses about what technology they support and how we should design the site.

Make Design Decisions

You can never control every variable that will go into how your user sees your Web site, but you should always try to consider the most important ones. Following are some things that might be considered when developing the three sample sites:

- Screen resolution—Defining the size of the screen/browser for which you will optimize your presentation. In cases where the screen layout is built to fit variable screen resolutions, this may be a range of screen sizes for which you will build and test.
- Color depth—The minimum resolution of your user. Pages render much differently in lower resolutions than they do in higher resolutions, especially when JPEGs are used to display pictures or when GIFs use non–Web-safe colors.

- Navigation—How the user will navigate the content and where the navigation exists in the interface is the most important design decision that needs to be made.
- Styles—Styles in the form of font face, color, and placement give the user visual clues that divide the content from the navigation. Styles also imply how the navigation functions and how the content is arranged. This often involves creating test layouts with fake information to get an idea of how things will look and flow.
- Plug-ins—By defining what plug-in technologies are to be used up front, you can simplify life for your developers, testers, and users.

Let's take a look at how we might make some design decisions on our three sample projects:

- Online catalog site—Because these users will be using modern equipment, the target screen resolution will be 800×600. Because of the number of full-color product shots the client wants to include, the users will need at least 16-bit color to view the site with clarity. This shouldn't be a problem with our target audience. The navigation chosen was a system of tabs up top, which relate to the four main areas of the print catalog, and an additional tab for company and contact information. No plug-ins are to be used with the site.
- Online training site—Because all the users in the company can view 1,024×800 content at 32-bit resolution, this was chosen as the minimum requirement for the site display. The navigation used will match the navigation that already exists on the intranet site; it will use a listing of topics and subtopics on the left side of the screen, which will be present on all pages. Because we know about the browser technology to be used, we're free to use Flash technology throughout the site to create illustrative animations.
- Poetry corner—Because users' screen sizes are likely to vary greatly, the site will be produced in a manner in which the content stretches to fill the screen. Target resolutions for testing will be 640×480, 800×600, and 1,024×768. Because the site has a creative edge to it and because it will be updated as a monthly "issue," the interface will use centrally connected links pulled together as hotspots on a main graphic. Sporadic use of plug-in technology will be made, including Macromedia Flash and Macromedia Shockwave. Links to download the plug-ins will be included on the main page and, depending on feedback, plug-in use will be increased or decreased.

Producing the Web Site

Based on an understanding of what the Web site is to do, who it is to be used by, and how it is to be designed, you are ready to begin producing your site. The timelines and resources involved vary from project to project, but in all cases, Dreamweaver will help you design, code, and maintain your site.

Dreamweaver helps you maintain the design of your site in CSS or HTML styles, which are reusable throughout your site and assure that all developers are applying the same look and feel. Tables and layers can be created, manipulated, and converted with a few mouse clicks, giving you the powerful capability to create your vision quickly. The capability to drag and drop objects in a GUI environment means that you can easily create several looks for your site for testing and approval.

Templates and library items can be used to centralize reusable elements in your pages, such as navigation and interface items. You can then easily update the templates and items and have all your changes replicated throughout the site.

Importance of Good Design and Navigation

The importance of good design cannot be overemphasized. Good design allows the maximum number of users to do what they need to do at your site, using the least amount of effort. Effort can be measured either in time at your site or the number of clicks. Anything that increases the number of clicks needed at your site or increases the amount of time needed to accomplish a task is burdensome to the design.

Common examples of this are the following:

- Navigation that is hidden in the interface
- Navigation that is unclear as to where it leads
- Common functions that are absent from the navigation
- Information that is divided needlessly over too many pages
- A lack of context clues, leading to users who feel "lost" in your site
- The need to log in at multiple points in a site
- Unclear directions for filling out forms

Although these design problems can be annoying for users of typical sites, for e-commerce sites they can be deadly. Consider what typical consumers go through when they walk into a retail store to make a purchase:

- Customers must have an understanding of what they are looking to do when they make a purchase—the need.
- Customers must be able to translate their need into a product that will solve the need.
- Customers must be able to locate the product within the store and make sure it is in inventory.
- Customers must be able to complete the sales transaction for the product using some form of currency that is accepted at the store.

For most of our real-world transactions, salespeople are available whose full-time job is to make sure the customer progresses from each level to the next. In the online world, on the other hand, this doesn't exist in the same fashion. For instance:

- If customers don't see your site as a place where they can solve their problems, they will leave.
- If your site doesn't help them translate their problem into a product they can buy, they will leave.

- If customers are not sure if your site carries the product or think it is not in stock, they will leave.
- If customers have problems filling out the necessary forms needed to complete the transaction, they will leave.

If the design of an e-commerce site fails at any of these levels, it will not make the sale. Worse, in most cases when customers leave, they just leave, and they usually will not take the time to explain why they left. Also, the likelihood that they will come back to your site in the future has been decreased or diminished altogether.

Design Tips and Tricks

Following are several helpful items to keep in mind when designing your site or to use when you get stuck in the process. Good design is both an art and a science, neither of which can be learned overnight.

Try Several Approaches

The best designs don't always happen in the first pass. Try several related designs before deciding on a single approach. If you still feel stuck, try standing the design on its head—change everything and see what you come up with.

Identify Your Users

Listing and describing the types of users who will be visiting your site will help you decide what to emphasize in the navigation and how to organize your materials. It will also help you streamline elements of your interface by asking yourself, "Just which type of user would want to go here?" about each of the sections of your navigation.

Consistently Use Styles

Lots of information is conveyed to your users through the use of text and graphical styles. Each new style that you add should have a specific new purpose. For instance, if you use boldface to emphasize some text and use a color change to emphasize other text, alert users will wonder why a style difference exists and what you are trying to convey. If the boldface and color change mean the same thing, you will be needlessly confusing your users.

Clarity in navigation of your site is an absolute necessity and is accomplished through the consistent and clear use of styles throughout your site. By interpreting the navigation and its styles on a site, users should always be able to tell where in a site they are and how to navigate in the direction they want to go.

Be Aware of Context

If your site is going to be used inside a larger site or in conjunction with another site, you should determine whether the styles and conventions of the other site are appropriate for use in your site. Doing so can save on development effort and be an aid to your users, who need to adjust only to a single interface style.

Also, it is much easier for new users to become "lost" in a site and become frustrated than it is for the people who designed the site. It's easy to think that your design is intuitive and perfect when you're the one who built it. Try your design on others before you become too self-confident about it. Also remember that many labels used for buttons can have more than one meaning, causing confusion for new users.

Summary

Designing a Web site for maximum usability is both an art and a science. In all cases, you'll need to start with an understanding of who your users are and why they are coming to your site. Next, you'll make decisions about the site itself and then complete the development of the site.

Sample Questions

1. When defining your audience, which factor would you probably not consider?
   A. The likelihood of users having the newest browser installed.
   B. The users' reasons for visiting the site.
   C. Screen resolution.
   D. You would consider all these factors.

2. True or False: If your site is to be part of a larger site, you should make the interface as different from that larger site as possible.

3. If users of an e-commerce site have trouble locating a product or completing a sale, they will most likely:
   A. Leave
   B. Call
   C. Come back frequently
   D. Recommend your site to others

CHAPTER 5

Page Properties

Understanding Page Setup

For each HTML page, sets of properties enable the browser to determine how to render some visual elements by default, and nonvisual settings enable search engines to find your pages. Using Macromedia Dreamweaver, these page properties are set in two ways:

- Using the Modify, Page Properties dialog box
- Using the View, Head Content menu item to display the head section in the Document window

Page Properties

The Page Properties dialog box enables you to set the following attributes for each HTML page:

- Title
- Background Image and Color
- Text and Link Colors
- Page Margins
- Document Encoding
- Tracing Image
- Image Transparency

Title

The title of an HTML page helps site visitors keep track of what they're viewing as they browse, and it identifies the page in the visitor's history and bookmark lists. If you don't title a page, Dreamweaver titles the page as Untitled Document. This title is used in the browser's title bar, the user's history list, and the bookmark and favorites lists.

You can set the document title in several ways:

- Choose Modify, Page Properties, or right-click a blank portion of the document and select Page Properties from the context menu.
- Choose View, Head Content.
- Change the title in the toolbar of the Document window.

Some search engines use the title to help browsers find Web sites, so you should make the title meaningful.

Setting the document title puts the text within the `<title>` block tag, which is found within the `<head>` block tag.

Background Image and Color

To define an image or color for the page background, use the Page Properties dialog box. The default background color is set to white (`#FFFFFF`). If you use both a background image and a background color, the color appears while the image downloads, and then the image covers up the color. If the background image contains any transparent pixels, the background.color shows through.

> **NOTE**
>
> #FFFFFF is called an RGB color. RGB (red, green, and blue) refers to a system for representing the colors to be used on a computer display. RGB values are expressed with six digits in hexadecimal format.

Dreamweaver repeats the background image if it does not fill the entire window, just as browsers do (called tiling).

> **TIP**
>
> Use cascading style sheets (CSS) to disable image tiling.

Setting the background image and color results in the addition of the bgcolor and background attributes of the `<body>` tag, as shown in the following example:

```
<body background="/images/Brand4/Background.gif" bgcolor="white">
```

Text and Link Colors

The Page Properties dialog box also enables you to set default colors for text, links, visited links, and active links. By default, Dreamweaver defaults text color to black.

> **NOTE**
>
> The active link color is the color that a link changes to while it's being clicked. Some Web browsers may not use the color you specify.

You can also choose a preset color scheme to define the page background and text colors. Choose Commands, Set Color Scheme, and then choose a background color and a color set for text and links.

> **NOTE**
> Color-blind people may find it difficult to see certain low-contrast combinations of text colors and background colors. Take care to test your selection.

Setting the text and link colors results in the use of the following attributes of the `<body>` tag: text, link, vlink, and alink. The following example sets hyperlinks to "003399", visited links to "003399", and active links to "cc9900" within an HTML page:

```
<body link="#003399" vlink="#003399" alink="#cc9900" text="#333333">
```

Page Margins

As in a document-processing program, page margins define the amount of space between the browser window and the text on the page. Following are the four settings for page margins in the Page Properties dialog box:

- Left Margin
- Top Margin
- Margin Width
- Margin Height

> **TIP**
> The left and top margin settings are used only for Microsoft Internet Explorer. Netscape Navigator ignores these values. Netscape Navigator instead uses the Margin Width and Margin Height settings. For best cross-browser results, provide values for all four margin values. To suppress margins, set all values to 0.

To view the margins within the Dreamweaver Document window, use the Preview in Browser feature.

Setting the margins within the Page Properties dialog box sets the leftmargin, topmargin, marginwidth, and marginheight attributes as amounts in pixels, as shown in the following example:

```
<body leftmargin="10" topmargin="10" marginwidth="10" marginheight="10">
```

Document Encoding

Document encoding specifies the encoding used for characters in the document as they are displayed in the browser. The default for English and Western European languages is Western. This setting is used in the following ways:

- Dreamweaver displays the document using the fonts you specify in Font Settings for the Western (Latin1) encoding.
- A browser displays the document using the fonts the browser specifies for the Western (Latin1) encoding.

The default encoding is stored with the document in a `<meta>` tag inserted within the `<head>` tag of the document. The `<meta>` tag for Western (Latin1) is the following:

```
<meta http-equiv="Content-Type" content="text/html; charset=iso-8859-1">
```

Tracing Images

A tracing image is a visual depiction of the site design created in a graphics application and imported into Dreamweaver. This graphic may either be a JPEG, a GIF, or a PNG file. This tracing image is placed in the background of the Document window. You can hide the image, set its opacity, and change its position. However, this image is only visible within Dreamweaver as a guide to create pages.

You can set the tracing image through the Page Properties dialog box as well as through the View, Tracing Image, Load menu items.

> **TIP**
>
> If you do not see the tracing image in the Document window, choose View, Tracing Image, Show.

Because tracing images are a design-time-only feature, no HTML is generated from their use.

Head Content

HTML files are made up of two main sections: the head and the body. The body section is the visible part of the document containing text and images. The head section is invisible, except for the document title.

The head section contains important information, including the following:

- Document title
- Meta properties
- Keyword and Description properties
- Refresh properties
- Scripts
- Base properties
- Link properties

You can view and set the elements in the head section using the Head Objects panel, the View menu, the Document window's Code view, or the Code Inspector.

Meta Properties

You've already seen the generation of the `<meta>` tag using document encoding. The creation and use of `<meta>` tags enable setting other page information, such as the author, the copyright, and keywords. It also sets information relevant to the server, such as the expiration date, the refresh interval, and the PICS rating for the page.

> **NOTE**
>
> PICS, the Platform for Internet Content Selection, provides a method for assigning ratings to Web pages.

The format of `<meta>` tags include the three attributes shown in Table 5.1:

Table 5.1 `<meta>` ***Tag Attributes***

Attribute Name	Description
`Name`	Specifies the `<meta>` tag; contains descriptive information about the page.
`Http-equiv`	Specifies the `<meta>` tag; contains HTTP header information.
`Value`	The type of information you're supplying to the tag. Descriptions, Keywords and Refresh are already predefined, but you can make up any value and associate a value using the Content attribute.
Content	The actual information that corresponds to the value.

Keywords and Descriptions

Using robots, search engine sites automatically browse the Web, gathering information to index. These robots use the contents of the Keywords and Description `<meta>` tags and use the information to index your pages in their databases. Description tags may also be used to display the information on the search results page. Choose a few relevant keywords and well-formed descriptions because some search engines have limitations on the number of keywords and length of descriptions they will use.

Creating keywords and descriptions creates `<meta>` tags, as in the following example:

```
<meta name="keywords" content="Macromedia Dreamweaver">
<meta name="description" content="Macromedia Dreamweaver
   is a design and development tool for Web professionals.">
```

Refresh

After a page is loaded into the browser, it remains static until a user makes another request. Using a `<meta>` tag, you can tell the browser to automatically refresh the current page or load a new page after a specified amount of time.

> **TIP**
>
> This element is often used to redirect users from one URL to another after displaying a text message that the URL has changed.

Set the Delay value, which is time in seconds to wait for refresh. To make the browser refresh the page immediately after it finishes loading, set this value to 0. Specify an Action—whether the browser should go to a different URL or refresh the current page after the specified delay.

Using a refresh creates a `<meta>` tag with the following attributes:

```
<meta http-equiv="refresh" content="10;URL=http://www.macromedia.com">
```

Base URL

Use the Base element to set the base URL that all document-relative paths in the page are considered relative to. The two settings available for this element are described in Table 5.2.

Table 5.2 Base Element

Setting	Description
Href	The base URL
Target	The frame or window in which all linked documents should open.

> **TIP**
>
> Base URLs are beneficial when you use framesets, because they allow you to specify a default target for your URLs.

Target values and where the new page gets loaded are listed in Table 5.3:

Table 5.3 Target Values

Value	Loads Linked Document To
framename	Specific frame in the frameset.
_blank	New, unnamed browser window.
_parent	Parent frameset or window of the frame that contains the link. If the frame containing the link is not nested, this is equivalent to _top; the linked document loads into the full browser window.
_self	Same frame or window as the link. This target is the default, so you usually don't have to specify it.
_top	Full browser window, thereby removing all frames.

Inserting a base URL generates a <base> tag within the <head> container tag. The following example sets all URLs relative to the file specified in the href attribute:

```
<base href="http://www.mysite.com/index.htm" target="_blank">
```

Link Information

Use the Link element to define a relationship between the current document and another file. This link is not a visual hyperlink between two pages. Instead, it creates links to style sheets or font definitions.

> **NOTE**
> There are other possible uses of linking, but they are not fully defined in the HTML 4.0 specification, nor do current browsers exploit them.

Linking a style sheet to an HTML document creates the <link> tag and locates it within the <head> block tag.

```
<link rel="stylesheet" href="../style_sheets/planner.css" type="text/css">
```

Summary

Page properties are created and stored within tags inside the <head> block tag and are set as attributes of the <body> tag. These settings enable page setup of visual settings as well as options to share information with search engine robots.

Sample Questions

1. Which <meta> tag name is used to display content in the results of a search engine search?
   A. Refresh
   B. Keyword
   C. Description
   D. Content

2. Which page margin settings are used by Microsoft Internet Explorer and ignored by Netscape Navigator? (Choose 2)
   A. Left
   B. Top
   C. Width
   D. Height

3. Which page property is not enabled through the <meta> tag?
   A. Left margin
   B. Keyword
   C. Description
   D. Title

PART II

BUILDING A WEB SITE

CHAPTER 6

Using Layers for Page Layout

Introduction

Effective page layout requires control over positioning of contents—especially horizontal positioning. The only means of controlling horizontal positioning in HTML alone is to use tables. The majority of pages on the Web today use tables, and the results are often very fine.

Complex page layouts require many tables, however, often requiring nested tables and many cells filled only with spacer images. The resulting code can be extremely complex, prone to syntax errors, difficult to debug, and difficult to read and maintain.

With layers and CSS positioning, an alternative way of laying out pages arrived. The code for pages laid out with layers is much simpler, consisting of a few `<div>` tags, because layers are designed for layout, whereas tables were forced into that role as an expediency. The complicated work of specifying positions is done—as it should be—by CSS.

Layers also provide possibilities not available for tables. They can be overlapped. In Internet Explorer and Netscape 6 and later, they can be nested. Layers can be animated using JavaScript to modify the CSS properties in response to events or the passage of time.

NOTE

If you might need to convert layers to tables later, you should not overlap layers. You can manually fix overlaps by moving layers. You can also prevent overlap of layers by choosing Modify, Arrange, Prevent Layer Overlaps or selecting the Prevent Overlaps option in the Layers panel.

Despite these advantages, layers are used relatively rarely for page layout on the Web. The reluctance of developers to employ them seems to result from concerns about browser support. Such concerns are often unfounded because the technologies needed for layers have now been supported by browsers for several years, and the number of users with nonsupporting browsers has dwindled to a very few, probably none for sites that attract technically informed users.

Dreamweaver's tools for creating and modifying layers make creation of page layouts very easy, without the need to switch to a special design mode. Layers also make it easy to set up templates, because the editable regions you need to create should correspond exactly to layers in the page layout.

For those who still want to deploy pages laid out with tables, layers can be converted into a table with a single command.

TIP

Dreamweaver enables you to create layers using the `<div>` tag or the `<layer>` (or `<ilayer>`) tag. The right choice is almost certainly the `<div>` tag. The `<layer>` and `<ilayer>` tags, introduced by Netscape with version 4.0, were not adopted into the HTML specification and are supported only by Netscape 4.x browsers.

Creating Layers

As with most elements, layers can be created in two ways in Dreamweaver:

- Click the Layer icon on the Common group in the Objects panel, and then click and drag to create a layer in the Document window.
- Select Insert, Layer, which will insert a layer into the document using the default layer properties defined in the Dreamweaver Preferences.

Layers and Tracing Images

Layers are particularly effective for page layout when you use them in conjunction with a tracing image. A tracing image is a GIF, JPG, or PNG image representing a page the way it will be viewed by a user. (Web developers are often given the task of reproducing such images, produced by a graphic designer, in an HTML page or template.) The tracing image can be attached to a page or template through the Page Properties.

> **TIP**
>
> It may be useful to set the Tracing Image Transparency to opaque while you create the template to match colors in the page mockup. After you have created the layout, however, you will probably want to remove the tracing image or reset the transparency of the tracing image to a lower value to avoid confusion over what objects exist in the page and image.

To create a page layout from a tracing image, you simply insert layers and then move and resize them to match the major content areas of the page. (Modifying layer properties is covered in the next section.) There is some art to the process. For instance, a navigation bar could be implemented in a page in more than one way: as separate layers for each navigation item or as a single layer that contains a table to hold the individual navigation elements. The right design choices will depend on the particular site and page, but a good general rule is the following: wherever you might conceivably want to create a separate template region for a nontechnical user to fill with content or to edit, you should have a separate layer.

Layer Properties

After it is inserted, a layer can be modified in several ways. To insert content into a layer, you simply click inside it to locate the cursor there and then add any content you want—any HTML element that can be added to the body can also be added to a `<div>` tag (including another nested `<div>` tag).

To select the layer itself, you can click the layer handle or border shown in the Design view, Ctrl+Shift+click inside the layer, or use the Tag Selector. Selecting a layer enables you to modify the layer properties.

For layers, unlike almost all other HTML elements, most of the properties exposed in the Property Inspector are not attributes of the tag, but CSS properties (width, height, left, top, visibility, and the like). These properties are attached to the `<div>` tag through the style attribute, but could just as well be defined in an ID or class rule in an embedded or linked style sheet.

> **NOTE**
>
> All CSS property values that define a length can be defined in terms of various physical or relative units, including px (pixels), in (inches), cm (centimeters), and pt (points).

The properties available for layers are discussed in the following subsections.

Layer ID

The layer ID uniquely identifies the layer for purposes of attaching an ID style rule or for scripting to modify the properties of the layer on a timeline or in response to an event. Dreamweaver provides unique IDs by default as layer1, layer2, and so on. If you assign your own IDs, you must make sure that they are unique within the page.

Tag

The drop-down menu lets you choose the <div>, <span>, <layer>, or <ilayer> tag to define the layer. For page layouts, <div> is almost always the best choice.

L (Left)

L (left) is a CSS property that defines the distance from the left edge of the page body (or the parent layer, if this is a nested layer) to the left edge of the layer.

T (Top)

T (top) is a CSS property that defines the distance from the top edge of the page body (or the parent layer, if this is a nested layer) to the top edge of the layer.

> **NOTE**
>
> Although they are not exposed in the Property Inspector, you can modify other CSS properties for the layer, such as padding and border, by adding properties in the Code view or defining an ID or class rule for it.

W (Width)

W (width) is a CSS property that defines the width of the layer.

H (Height)

H (height) is a CSS property that defines the height of the layer.

Z-Index

The CSS z-index property defines the stacking order of layers. Z-index is a positive integer value, and layers with higher z-index values appear on top of layers with lower values.

By default, Dreamweaver assigns higher z-index values to overlapping layers as they are created, but it does not automatically change z-index values when you overlap existing panels by moving them in Design view. If overlapping layers have the same z-index value, the one that appears first in the list of layers in the Layers panel will appear on top of subsequent layers in the list.

> **TIP**
>
> Do not rely on the ordering of panels in the Layers panel to define stacking order. If you use overlapping layers, define the z-index values explicitly to define the stacking order.

Z-index values can be changed in the Layers panel as well as in the Property Inspector.

Vis (Visibility)

Visibility, a CSS property, defines whether the layer is visible, hidden, or inherits the visibility of its parent element. Visibility will normally be set to visible or default (which should also be visible) for layers that are used for page layout. There is no obvious reason to create invisible layers unless you are going to provide a mechanism for changing the visibility via scripting that is attached to a timeline or launched by some event.

Overflow

The CSS overflow property controls how contents are handled when they overflow the boundaries of the layer (defined by the width and height properties). The options are visible, hidden, scroll, and auto (which means the browser's default value, which is likely to be "visible").

This is a very important property for layers that will form editable regions of a template. If you want to constrain content to the boundaries of the layer (to prevent users with your target display resolution from having to scroll to see the entire page), you will need to educate content providers using the template about keeping content within the layer because Dreamweaver will not enforce this. If, on the other hand, you want to allow overflow by setting the property to visible or auto, you need to make sure that no content is below the frame that the overflow would overlap with.

Bg Image (Background-Image)

The CSS background-image property allows you to specify any GIF, JPG, or PNG file as a background image for the layer.

> **TIP**
>
> Remember that background images in CSS need not be tiled across the whole background of the element, as they are in HTML. Instead, the image can be tiled only vertically or horizontally or appear only once. To use these features of CSS, you will need to manually edit the style value for the `<div>` tag in the Code view.

Bg Color (Background-Color)

The CSS background-color property sets a background color for the layer. This, like the background-image property, has the effect of rendering the layer opaque, so that it will conceal any contents that are beneath it.

Clip

The CSS clip property enables you to specify a rectangular region within the layer that is visible, rendering any content outside the clip region as hidden. Clip settings are primarily used for special graphical effects.

Summary

Layers provide an alternative to page layout that can be achieved with much more compact code. You can draw layers in a page using the Object panel or insert layers with default properties through the Insert menu. Layer properties can be modified through the Property Inspector; some properties can also be modified through the Layers panel. The important properties for layers are CSS properties rather than HTML attributes.

Sample Questions

1. What property controls the stacking order of overlapping layers?
   A. Overflow
   B. Z-index
   C. Visibility
   D. Stacking-Order

2. To convert layers to a table, what must be true of a page layout made with layers?
   A. No CSS properties are used to define the layers.
   B. The visibility of all layers must be set to visible.
   C. The layers must not overlap.
   D. The layers must have unique layer IDs.

CHAPTER 7

Using Tables for Page Layout

What Are Tables?

Tables have two primary purposes in HTML files. One is to display formatted information in the form of a chart on the page; the other is to aid in the design and layout of a page. In both cases they use the same set of tags, but how they are created and manipulated differs within Macromedia Dreamweaver.

When viewed in a browser or in the design pane, tables are divided into columns and rows, forming a grid of cells. The division between each cell is marked with an optional border. In Dreamweaver, a dotted line is shown when the border is hidden. In some cases, cells can expand to fill more than one column or row. Tables and the height and width of cells can be sized. Sizes can be described as a percentage of the space available (also called relative sizing) or as a fixed size in pixels (also called absolute sizing.) It is common to use a combination of both approaches to achieve the desired effect.

Table cells can contain any valid HTML content, including other tables. For objects contained within a table cell, all relative sizing depends on the space available in the cell. Centering, for instance, positions the object based on the left and right sides of the cell, rather than on the left and right sides of the page, as it would when the object was not contained within a table. If the content in a cell is larger than the space allocated to the cell, the cell will be expanded either horizontally, vertically, or in both directions.

When tables are used to create simple charts for information, they are usually filled with text information and frequently use colored backgrounds to help the user interpret the information. In these cases, tables should always contain a description in the form of a value for the summary attribute. This will allow those using nonvisual browsers to interpret the overall meaning of the table. This attribute needs to be set in the Code view, Code Inspector, or Quick Tag Editor because the Property Inspector does not currently support this attribute.

When tables are used to manage the layout of information on a page, they will frequently be used to fill a fixed area (based on the viewable area of the target browser sizes) or will be used to fill a large percentage of the browser window. In the latter case, a single column of information is usually chosen to expand and shrink with the table, which is called the autostretch column in Dreamweaver. This column usually contains mostly text information, which can be formatted to stretch and shrink within an expandable cell.

Inserting Tables in Standard View

Tables are inserted in Dreamweaver in the Standard view by either choosing Insert, Table from the menu or by selecting the Table object from the Objects panel. Dreamweaver will ask you for some basic information about the table when you do this, including the following:

- Rows—The number of rows in the table.
- Columns—The number of columns in the table.
- Width—The total width of the table. This can be expressed either as pixels (fixed width) or as a percentage (relative width).
- Border—The width or height of the border around the table and each cell.
- Cell Padding—The amount of space, in pixels, between the contents of the cell and its border. Setting this to `0` means that content will be pushed right up against the border of the cell.
- Cell Spacing—The amount of space, in pixels, between each cell. Setting this to `0` means that cells will be flush against each other, leaving room only for the border if it exists.

Table Code

A simple table in Dreamweaver with only a single cell might look like the following:

```
<table width="100%" border="1">
    <tr>
        <td>Duke</td>
    </tr>
</table>
```

The preceding code would create a table spanning 100% of its available space. The available space would be determined by the object in which the table was contained, such as the page, frame, or table cell. A more complicated table might have multiple rows and columns. This might look like the following:

```
<table width="350" border="1" align="center">
    <tr bgcolor="#FFFF33">
        <td>Rene Magritte</td>
        <td>Salvador Dali</td>
    </tr>
    <tr bgcolor="#FF0033">
        <td>Andy Warhol</td>
        <td>James Rosenquist</td>
    </tr>
    <tr bgcolor="#FFFF33">
        <td>Keith Haring</td>
        <td>Roy Lichtenstein</td>
    </tr>
</table>
```

The preceding code would create a table that takes up exactly 350 pixels in width and is aligned to the center of the space containing it. The table has two columns and three rows, each of which alternates in color.

Any table requires at least three tags—`<table>`, `<tr>`, and `<td>`—to be nested within each other in the order shown in the example. Each set of tags signifies a different level of properties within the table:

- `<table>`—This set of tags signifies the start and the end of the table. Its properties are used to determine how wide the table is as a whole, the default background color of the table cells, the border width and color, cell padding, cell spacing, and alignment within its containing object.
- `<tr>`—This set of tags signifies a row within the table. A table can have multiple sets of `<tr>` tags; each `<tr>` tag represents a new row in the table.
- `<td>`—This tag signifies a unique data cell within the row. A `<tr>` tag can have multiple `<td>` tags; each `<td>` tag represents a new column in the row. In most cases, the number of TD tags will be the same in every row.

Selecting Table Elements

You can use several ways to select cells in Dreamweaver. Depending on what you are trying to select and what you are trying to change, you may find each method more or less useful.

Selecting a Cell

One way to select a cell in Dreamweaver is to place the cursor inside it and then choose Edit, Select All, or use Ctrl+A (or Command+A on the Macintosh). This will select the cell and allow you to change its properties in the Properties Inspector.

Another way to select a cell is to put your cursor inside the cell and to select the `<td>` tag from the tag selector. The Tag Selector is the recursively listed selection of tags that show your position in HTML. It is located in the bottom-left corner of the Document window.

Selecting Several Cells

Several adjacent cells can be selected by clicking in a cell and dragging in any direction within the table. All cells between the start cell and the end cell will be selected, in a rectangular fashion. If you do not want to select a full rectangle of cells, or if the cells you want to select are nonadjacent, you can select individual cells by holding down the Ctrl key while selecting the cells you want to select.

Selecting Columns or Rows

Entire columns or rows can be selected by clicking the very top of the table at the border above the column you want to select, or on the left border, you can select an entire row. Your cursor will turn into a down arrow or a right arrow when you are in the correct spot. If you want to select multiple columns and rows, you can click and drag. If you want to select nonadjacent rows or columns or mix and match your selection between rows and columns, you can hold down the Ctrl key while clicking.

Selecting an Entire Table

You can select an entire table by clicking inside the table you want to select and pressing Ctrl+A to select the cell; then select Control+A again to select the table. You can also select the entire table by clicking inside any cell and using the Tag Selector to select the `<table>` tag. A table can also be selected with the mouse by clicking to the left or right of the table and dragging onto the table.

Modifying Table Elements

After you have the table or some of its parts selected, you can change various properties of the cell, row, or table in the Properties Inspector. Additionally, any text formatting you make at this point will be applied only to the cells you have selected.

When you have cells selected, you can make the following changes directly from the Properties Inspector:

- Horizontal Positioning—How the contents of the cell will be positioned horizontally. By default, this value pushes the content to the left.
- Vertical Positioning—How the contents of the cell will be positioned vertically. By default, this value pushes the content to the center.
- Width—The width of the individual cell. Because of differences in how browsers render tables, all cells in a column should have the same width setting.
- Height—The height of the cell and, in most cases, the height of the row.
- No Wrap—A setting that keeps the browser from automatically wrapping text to keep within the designated width of the column. As a result, text can cause the column to extend past its defined value.
- Header—A setting that applies the default properties of a header to the cell. In most cases, this applies bold and centers the content. Used to quickly separate labels from data in charts. It also changes the code to use the `<th>` tag instead of the `<td>` tag.

- Background Image—An image that is to appear behind the cell.
- Background Color—The color of the background in the cell.
- Border—The border color for the cell.

When you have table cells selected, you can also perform the following functions through the Properties Inspector:

- Split Cell—This enables you to divide a cell into multiple cells, either in Rows or Columns.
- Merge Cells—This enables you to merge adjacent cells into one. Cells must be in either the same Column or Row.

When you have an entire table selected, you can modify the following properties:

- Width—The width of the entire table. Expressed either as pixels (fixed) or as a percentage (relative).
- Height—The height of the table. Expressed either as pixels or as a percentage.
- Cell Padding—The amount of space, in pixels, between the contents of the cell and its border. Setting this to `0` means that content will be pushed right up against the border of the cell.
- Cell Spacing—The amount of space, in pixels, between each cell. Setting this to `0` means that cells will be flush against each other, leaving room only for the border if it exists.
- Alignment—The relative position of the table in its container. Usually this is the page, but it may be a frame or another table cell.
- Border—The width of the table border in pixels.
- Border Color—The border color for the table.
- Background Image—An image that is to appear behind the table.
- Background Color—The color of the background in the table.

The following functions are available to you in the Properties Inspector when you have a table selected:

- Clear Row Heights—Strips out any height settings from the table cells.
- Clear Column Widths—Strips out any width setting from the table cells.
- Convert Table Widths to Pixels—Takes the current table widths in the Design view and codes each cell to exactly that many pixels in width.
- Convert Table Widths to Percentages—Takes each of the current table widths in the Design view and codes each cell to take up that same relative percentage in width.

Importing Tabular Data

Data for tables can be imported from text files generated from a variety of applications. When imported, the data will become a table within Dreamweaver that can then be sorted and formatted. To import data from a text file, select File, Import, Import Tabular Data. This opens a dialog box that enables you to specify which file you want to import, how the data is formatted, and how it should appear within Dreamweaver when you are done.

The Import Table dialog box enables you to fill out the following:

- Data File—The source document that contains the data to be imported. This will have been generated by some external application, such as Excel, Access, Filemaker Pro, and so on, or it could have been created by hand using a simple text editor. Most applications that hold or manipulate data have options for exporting that data in a variety of formats. You will want to export your selected data in a text format using one of the valid delimiters acceptable to Dreamweaver (see the following item). Because all applications work slightly differently, it is common to have to export the data several times until you find the setting that works the best. Note that each row of data (also sometimes called a record) must end with a paragraph marker.
- Delimiter—This is the single character that separates each item of data in a row. Standard delimiters are Tab, Comma, Semicolon, and Colon. You will want to use a delimiter that is not otherwise used in your data, because this can cause Dreamweaver to unnecessarily divide cells and to add extra columns to your resulting table. If you are using a character that is not a standard delimiter, you can choose Other as the delimiter to reveal a text entry box that allows you to enter your custom delimiter. Note that you can enter only a single character in this box; multiple character delimiters must be edited either before importation in a text editor or after importation using Find and Replace.
- Table Width—The default width of the table can be set either to adjust itself to the data or to use a standard percentage or pixel value. Adjusting to data really means that the table will be built without width information embedded in it and will therefore adjust itself naturally to the data size when it is rendered in a browser.
- Format Top Row—Enables you to select how the top row will be formatted in the table. The first record, which becomes the top row, is often used to hold labels for the data in many text-based data formats. If this is the case for the data you are importing, you may want to format it using some combination of bold and italic, which are available in the pull-down menu.
- Cell Padding—The amount of space, in pixels, between the contents of the cell and its border. Setting this to `0` means that content will be pushed right up against the border of the cell.
- Cell Spacing—The amount of space, in pixels, between each cell. Setting this to `0` means that cells will be flush against each other, leaving room only for the border if it exists.
- Border—The width of the border in pixels. For no border, use zero (`0`).

After you have selected the file to import, how it is formatted, and how it should be displayed on the page, you can click the OK button to import the data as a table. The table will be imported into the area selected by your cursor and will be selected. You can then manipulate the table using any available method. After data is imported into a page as a table, it is no longer linked to the external file. Changes to the external file will not be reflected in the HTML document.

Sort Table

To sort a table (either one that was a result of importing a data file or one that was created within Dreamweaver), you place the cursor inside the table and choose Commands, Sort Table. This will bring up the Sort Table dialog box, which enables you to specify how the table is to be sorted.

The Sort Table feature enables you to specify a primary and a secondary column to sort by. Dreamweaver uses the first sort order to organize the rows into a new order and the second to order any rows that match in the first specified column. A common example of this is sorting by last name and first name, in which listed names would be organized first by last name in alphabetical order and then ordered within each last name by first name. The second sorting order is optional in this feature and can be omitted.

The two sort orders enable you to specify the following:

- Sort By—This identifies the column that should be sorted. You identify the column by number, with the first column being the first on the left. The pull-down menu should give you as many options as there are columns in the table you have selected.
- Order—This specifies how the sorting should be done, either alphabetically or numerically. Alphabetical sorts work from left to right within the cell, ordering each item based on its relative position in the alphabet (regardless of case). Numbers in an alphabetical sort are treated based on their ASCII value, meaning that they come before letters but after other symbols, such as commas and quotes. Sorting columns of numbers alphabetically will cause erratic results because 100 will be considered to come before 9. Numerically ordered sorts treat each value as a number and sorts according to its real value. Letters are ordered after numbers, and characters are ordered before numbers.
- Direction—The direction of the sort can be either Ascending or Descending. The default direction is ascending. Switching the direction to descending reverses the rules for the sort, causing rows that would come later in the table to come first.

Two options also are available to you to alter how the table is sorted:

- Sort Includes First Row—Frequently, the first row of data that you are formatting includes headers describing what each column contains. In these cases, you would not want to include the first row in your sorting. If the first row does not contain data, you probably would want to include it in your sorting, in which case you would want to make sure this option is checked.
- Keep TR Attributes with Sorted Row—Frequently, formatting applied to tables is done for clarity, such as when alternate rows of a table are colored. In these cases, you would not want to move the row attributes with the sorted data; this would ruin the readability of the table. If the row level formatting is important to the data in the row, such as when highlighting abnormalities in the data, you would want to make sure this option is checked.

Format Table

To quickly format tables in Dreamweaver into pleasant-looking charts, use the Format Table command; place the cursor inside a table and select Commands, Format Table from the menu. This feature allows you to format an existing table using one of 16 predefined styles. Each style is also customizable to fit your needs.

The Format Table dialog box shows a sample table that allows you to preview the style and changes you make to it. Other options in this dialog box include those shown in Table 7.1.

Table 7.1 Options in the Format Table Dialog Box

Option	Description
Row Colors	Enables you to set the two colors that will be used to stripe your data.
Alternate	Enables you to set the pacing with which the row colors will be alternated. You can select a frequency of 1, 2, 3, 4, or not to alternate the colors.
Top Row Align	Allows you to pick the alignment for the top row, should this contain labels for your columns.
Top Row Text Style	Allows you to pick a text style for your top row.
Top Row Background Color	Enables you to choose the background color of the top row.
Top Row Text Color	Enables you to specify a text color for the top row.
Left Column Align	Enables you to specify an alignment for your left column, should it contain labels for each row of data.
Left Column Text Style	Enables you to set a style for the left column of text.
Border	Enables you to specify a border size for your table, shown between each of the cells and around the table.
Apply All Attributes to TD Tags Instead of TR Tags	This option, if checked, has Dreamweaver apply the row-specific attributes to each cell instead of centralizing them inside the row tag.

Table Layout View

> **NOTE**
>
> The Layout View mode is a powerful new option introduced in Dreamweaver 4. If you are used to creating layouts using the regular table tools in Dreamweaver, you should take some time and learn this new method.

Layout view enables you to manipulate tables in a more visual manner. With this mode you are free to create tables, add content into cells, and freely manipulate the properties of the cells as if they are independent, positional objects. Dreamweaver will maintain the table code, creating columns, rows, and manipulating the properties of the cells to create HTML that displays content based on the design you have developed. The functionality of the Layout mode matches that of the Layers tools within Dreamweaver, but without the traditional problems related to deploying pages containing layers. Additionally, you can use Dreamweaver to convert layouts done with layers into tables or convert a table back into layers.

To enter the Layout view, you change the View setting in the Objects panel to Layout View. When you do this, you will notice that two options are now available to you: Layout Cells and Layout Table. You will also notice that the Table and Layer objects become unavailable to you in the Objects panel. These objects will return to their active state when you return to the Standard view. While in the Layout view, you will not be able to create layers, and you will create tables using the layout tools.

Layout Tables

You can create a new layout table by selecting either of the Layout Cell or Layout Table tools. Using the Layout Table allows you to define the exact size of the table you will use. The Layout Cell tool is then used to draw cells within the table you have created. If you draw a cell in an area where there is no table, one will be created for you.

Each layout table on the page is clearly marked with the text Layout Table. Along the top of the bar, broken at each column, is a button showing the pixel width for that column. Clicking the Width button will reveal a pull-down menu that allows certain formatting problems to be fixed.

Adding Cells and Content in Layout View

> **TIP**
>
> You can also load a tracing image for use in your table design. This allows you to temporarily bring in a background image and to precisely draw your cells on top.

Cells are added to Layout Tables by choosing the Layout Cell object from the Objects panel. To use this tool, you click a corner and drag to create a new cell with content inside a Layout Table. The tool tends to "stick" to existing corners and borders, but it can be used to create a cell floating anywhere within the layout table.

After a cell is created, it will turn from gray to white, which means that it is open for the addition of content. Any content can be added to the layout tables, including other layout tables.

> **TIP**
>
> Adding layout tables inside layout tables can make the interface tricky to edit and maintain. You are usually better off just creating additional cells within the larger table. If you decide to nest your layout tables within each other, make sure you have a good reason to do it.

Content can be typed in and formatted using the regular Dreamweaver tools. It can also be imported and grabbed from the site library. You can do practically everything you would do to format content in this mode except create tables with the Table object and add layers to your file.

Manipulating Cells in Layout View

One of the most powerful features of the Layout Table view is its capability to allow manipulation of cells without worrying about how it will impact your code. Dreamweaver will create, manipulate, and destroy columns and rows to make your design work as close to the way you have built it as possible. To select a cell, do one of the following:

- Click in the cell and select Edit, Select All to select the cell.
- Click in the cell and select TD from the Tag Selector at the bottom of the Document window.
- Click the outer edge of a content cell.

In all cases, you should see a border appear around the edge of the cell with grow handles on each corner and each side. You can manipulate the size of a cell by clicking a grow handle and dragging it in or out. Using the grow handles on the sides will limit your changes to a single dimension at a time.

To move the cell, you can do two things:

- Click the edge of the cell (not on a grow handle) and drag the cell to the new position. Your cursor will change to an arrow when it is positioned correctly.
- Press the arrow keys in the direction you want to move the cell. You should see the cell move one pixel at a time.

When you have a Layout Cell selected, you can manipulate several properties in the Properties Inspector, including those shown in Table 7.2.

Table 7.2 Options in the Layout Cell Property Inspector

Property	Description
Width	The width of the individual cell. Notice that your options are a fixed number of pixels and autostretch. Dreamweaver doesn't like to use relative sizing for most table columns unless the cell is made to autostretch. Autostretching is explained later in this chapter.
Height	The height of the individual cell.
Background Color	The color of the background in the cell.
Horizontal Positioning	How the contents of the cell will be positioned horizontally. By default, this value pushes the content to the left.
Vertical Positioning	How the contents of the cell will be positioned vertically. By default, this value pushes the content to the center.
No Wrap	A setting that keeps the browser from automatically wrapping text to keep within the designated width of the column. As a result, text can cause the column to extend past its defined value.

Manipulating Layout Tables

You can select the whole table by doing one of the following:

- Place the cursor inside the table in a cell and press Ctrl+A to select the Cell; press Control+A again to select the table.
- Place the cursor inside the table in a cell and click the Table tag in the Tag Selector.
- Click the green Table Layout label at the top of the layout table.

After you have selected the table, you will see three grow handles. One is in the lower-right corner, one is on the right side, and one is on the bottom of the table. Each grow handle allows you to manipulate the size of the table. Notice that no grow handles are on the top on the right sides of the table. The table itself is a regular HTML object and cannot be positioned like cells or layers can. This means you may need to leave space on the left side or top side to give the effect of your content floating on the page. Fortunately, Dreamweaver makes this very easy to do.

Autostretching

When you create a new layout table, it is created with a fixed width. Frequently, you will change the width to match the target browser size for the project you are working on. Sometimes you will want to target variable browser sizes and want the content to flow into whatever size it is viewed. When this happens, you want to use the autostretching feature of Dreamweaver. Autostretching enables you to identify a single column that expands or shrinks, based on the user's browser window and the content being displayed. This gives the effect that the content is being customized for any given browser window—all within a single file.

To turn on autostretching, you figure out which column you want to stretch and click the Width button above that column. From the pull-down menu, select the Make Column Autostretch menu item.

> **NOTE**
>
> When you add a spacer image, Dreamweaver creates a file called spacer.gif or asks you to identify a file that should be used in its place. spacer.gif is a simple 1×1 transparent gif. Because browsers are more precise when sizing images than they are with table cells, adding a row of spacer images to the bottom of your table will force browsers to maintain your design better.

Sometimes when autostretching a table, you will need to return to the pull-down menu and choose Add Spacer Image. This action adds an extra row to your Layout Table with a height of 1, filled with properly sized spacer images. These are small invisible GIF files that size themselves to force your columns to draw with the correct widths. If you are using autostretching and notice that some of your columns are sized wrong in the browser, you should add these spacer images.

Converting Layers to Tables

Layers and Layout Tables are both powerful layout tools in Dreamweaver that can be used to create complex designs quickly and easily. Not surprisingly, because some people favor one tool or the other, or because of technology concerns, it is sometimes necessary to convert from one format into another. Although the code behind these two technologies looks very different, Dreamweaver can convert layers into tables that will appear almost the same as the layers did. It can also convert tables into layers as well. To convert layers into tables, do the following:

1. Open a file containing layers.
2. Make sure you are in the Standard view.
3. Choose Modify, Convert, Layers to Table.

To convert tables to layers, do the following:

1. Open a file containing at least one table.
2. Make sure you are in the Standard view.
3. Choose Modify, Convert, Tables to Layers.

Summary

Tables are a useful HTML device for formatting charts and for creating and maintaining design layout. Tables contain rows, which in turn contain data cells. Columns are made up from the alignment of data cells across rows.

Dreamweaver provides tools for creating and manipulating tables quickly. Dreamweaver can also generate tables from imported tabular data. Any table in Dreamweaver can be sorted and quickly formatted using built-in tools.

When using table layout tools, Dreamweaver gives us maximum control over each cell. Columns and rows are created and destroyed in order to maintain the layout automatically. Autostretching a column in this mode allows your design to stretch across the entire browser.

Layers can also be used for layouts and can be converted into tables when positioned properly. Inversely, tables can be converted back into layers at any point.

Sample Questions

1. Tabular data is imported as:
   A. Excel format
   B. Delimited text format
   C. Fixed-field records
   D. FileMaker Pro format

2. Autostretching works best with:
   A. Hidden spacer graphics
   B. Layers
   C. Charts and graphs
   D. Large image files

CHAPTER 8

Adding Basic Content

Adding Text

Simple text can be added to a document by placing your cursor in the Design view and typing. As you type, the characters are added to the code and displayed in turn in the Design view. Some characters that could be confused with HTML codes are replaced with equivalents so that the browser has an easier time rendering the code. The greater-than and less-than signs, for instance, are used to start and end HTML tags and, as a result, are replaced with `>` and `<` in the code when you type them in the Design view.

> **TIP**
>
> To enter these symbols directly without the symbols being converted, open the Code view and type directly into the code.

Text can also be pasted directly into Macromedia Dreamweaver. This is usually done by copying the file in the desired program and pasting the text into the desired location in the document. If the text is in plain ASCII text format, you can also open the file directly in Dreamweaver, copy the text, and paste it into your document.

> **TIP**
>
> By default, pasting text into Dreamweaver is similar to typing text, because it gets interpreted and special characters get replaced. To have Dreamweaver paste in the text directly so that it is not interpreted (such as when the text contains HTML code), use the Edit, Paste HTML option.

Paragraphs

By default, each time you press the Enter key, Dreamweaver creates a new paragraph. If you are typing text that doesn't already include paragraph markers at the beginning and at the end, Dreamweaver adds them to the previous paragraph when it creates the new paragraph. This is so that the text will be seen the same across browsers and so that any cascading style sheets that affect the <p> tag are applied to all your text.

> **NOTE**
>
> When working on sites that were originally designed in tools other than Dreamweaver, you may find the use of paragraph tags inconsistent. All paragraphs should begin with a <p> tag and end with a </p> tag. Leaving out the </p> tag or using the <p> tag only to separate paragraphs is considered invalid HTML. Where possible, it's a good idea to fix them or to have Dreamweaver fix them. HTML and XHTML standards are becoming less forgiving about inconsistently applied tags.

Headings

Headings enable passages of text to be divided and labeled in a logical manner. There are six heading tags, each of which refers to the level of the item in an outline. Because of this, the higher the number, the smaller the font size used to display the header. Heading tags are similar to paragraph tags in that one tag goes at the beginning and one at the end, with a small amount of space between the header and its preceding content and following content.

Heading tags are created by selecting an existing paragraph and choosing Text, Paragraph Format, Heading x, where *x* is the level of the heading. Paragraphs can also be converted into headings by changing the Format in the Properties Inspector.

Ordered and Unordered Lists

Most lists take two common forms: ordered lists and unordered lists, which use the tags `<ol>` and `<ul>`, respectively. Ordered lists refer to sets of numbered items, usually in order. Unordered lists, also commonly called bullet lists, use a marker, such as a bullet or square, to separate each item in the list. Both lists are made up of list items that use the `<li>` tag. Lists are created by selecting a set of existing paragraphs and choosing the correct list type from the Text, List submenu. You can also create lists by selecting paragraphs and clicking the Ordered List or Unordered List button in the Properties Inspector. Each button converts the currently selected text into a list using either numbers or bullets, as appropriate.

Lists can be nested within other lists by selecting a subset of items and choosing the Text Indent button in the Properties Inspector. Ordered lists that are nested use their own numbering, starting at 1.

NOTE

A less-common form of list is the Definition list. This list type alternates terms, which are placed flush right, with definitions, which are indented. These lists are commonly used to format lists of glossary terms.

Line Breaks

Although paragraph tags add extra lines between paragraphs for clarity, it is sometimes necessary to break a line without adding this much space. The line break, or `<br>` tag, is used for this function. To add a line break in Dreamweaver, you can hold down the Shift key as you press Enter, or you can use the Line Break object in the Characters category of the Objects panel.

TIP

Line breaks should be used only in passages of text that are contained in paragraph markers (`<p>`), headers (`<h1>`,`<h2>`, and so on), list items (`<li>`), or table cells (`<td>`). Other than these tags, line breaks may be inconsistently applied or ignored.

Properties Inspector

When dealing with text, the Properties Inspector is used to modify text after it has been entered or to change the way new text is to be created. All functions in the Properties Inspector are also available in the Text menu.

Format

The format of the text passage is set for the entire text line. It enables you to assign either a paragraph or heading style to the line. You can also designate Preformatted to designate a passage in which line breaks have been added. Formatting uses the `<p>`, `<pre>`, `<h1>`, `<h2>`, `<h3>`, `<h4>`, `<h5>`, or `<h6>` tags.

Font

The font is the character set used to represent the text on the page. Because different fonts are available on different systems, you can specify a list of fonts that may be used for the passage. Font is stored inside the `face` attribute of the `<font>` tag.

Size

The size of the font is a relative measurement ranging from 1, for the smallest font size, to 7, for the largest. Relative units, such as +2 and –1 can also be specified. To remove size information, select None from the pull-down menu. Size is stored in the `size` attribute of the `<font>` tag.

Color

The color of the font is the named or hexadecimal equivalent of the desired color. To remove the color information, select the Default Color button from the color pop-up. Color is stored in the `color` attribute of the `<font>` tag.

Style (Bold and Italic)

The two available styles in the Properties Inspector are Bold and Italicize. For additional styles, such as Underline, use the Text, Style submenu. Each style uses its own tag to start and end the style, such as the `<b>` tag for bold and the `<i>` tag for italic.

Justification

Justification enables you to specify Left, Center, or Right justification for the paragraph or heading. Justification is mutually exclusive. To remove justification after it has been selected, click the selected justification a second time. Justification is stored inside the `align` attribute of the related formatting tag (`<p>`, `<pre>`, or the heading tag).

Link and Target

Link and Target enable you to specify a new document (relative or absolute path) and the frame into which the document should be loaded. To remove link and target information, delete the text from the appropriate box. Link is stored inside the `href` attribute of the `<a>` tag. Target is stored inside the `target` attribute of the `<a>` tag.

Lists (Ordered and Unordered)

Ordered and Unordered List buttons enable you to turn the selected paragraphs into either ordered or unordered lists. Each line can be only one or the other. To remove the list setting, select the line or lines and click the List button a second time. Each list item uses `<li>` and `</li>` tags to replace `<p>` and `</p>` tags. The entire list is surrounded by either `<ol>` and `</ol>` tags for ordered lists or `<ul>` and `</ul>` tags for unordered lists.

Text Indent and Outdent

These options enable you to change the indenting of a particular passage. Dreamweaver adds or removes tags, depending on what items are selected. Using these options on lists, for instance, causes them to become nested or unnested. Using these options on normal paragraphs uses the `<blockquote>` tag.

Horizontal Rules

Horizontal rules are lines that divide sections of an HTML document. Their main purpose is to provide a visual clue to the user that information in the same document is supposed to be separate for some reason.

Horizontal rules can be selected and have their own properties in the Properties Inspector. The following properties can be changed:

- Width—Width in pixels or as a percentage of the container
- Height—Height in pixels

- Alignment—`Left`, `Center`, `Right`, or `Default` setting to justify the rule
- Shading—Allows the rule to be shaded

> **TIP**
>
> Horizontal rules are objects that use the `<hr>` tag. If you want to add color to the `<hr>` tag, you can do it with the `color` attribute in the quick editor. For even better results, it is recommended that you use cascading style sheets to color all `<hr>` tags in your site at the same time.

Special Characters

Special HTML characters that are part of the HTML standard are available through the Characters category of the Objects panel. All these characters are also available through the Insert, Special Characters submenu.

The two most common are the line break and the non-breaking space. The line break was discussed earlier in this chapter. The non-breaking space is commonly used as a placeholder to force paragraphs and table cells to draw correctly.

Other special characters are commonly used symbols for which no single keyboard equivalents exist. The most commonly used of these are Copyright, Registered, Left Quote, Right Quote, and Em Dash. For other special characters, use the Other object, which brings up the Insert Other Character dialog box, displaying the full assortment of nonstandard characters and symbols.

When a special character is inserted, Dreamweaver represents the character with a special code. The code always begins with an ampersand (&) and ends with a semicolon. In between is a set of letters or numbers that represent a predetermined symbol or character. This notation system allows HTML code to be more portable across different platforms.

HTML Styles Panel

The HTML Styles panel provides a way to build a set of reusable styles that can be used throughout your site. HTML styles are a Dreamweaver way to bind together various HTML calls that affect fonts and paragraphs.

> **NOTE**
>
> HTML styles work similarly to cascading style sheets but have two important differences. First, older browsers can understand them because they are implemented with regular HTML. Second, although they can be used to quickly apply styles throughout a site, they cannot be used to maintain common styles. If you update the definition of the style, you must go back to each use and reapply it.

The HTML Styles panel is opened with the Window, HTML Styles menu option. This displays all available styles. By default, two styles already exist in every site: Clear Selection Style and Clear Paragraph Style. The first clears all font styles from the selected passage, and the latter clears all font styles from the selected paragraph or heading.

To create a new style, click the New Style button in the lower corner of the panel. The Define New Style dialog box contains the following options:

- Name—The name of the style.
- Apply To—Sets whether the attributes should be applied to the selection or to the whole paragraph.
- When Applying—Sets whether previous styles should be removed.
- Font Attributes—Allows setting of the Font, Size, Color, and Styles for the selected passage.
- Paragraph Attributes—Allows setting of the Format and Alignment of the paragraph.

To apply an HTML style after it has been created, select the passage and click the style name from the HTML Styles panel. HTML styles are reusable throughout the site and are stored in XML format in a file called styles.xml in the Library folder.

Summary

Basic page content in the form of text and simple objects can be added and maintained through Dreamweaver. Headings, lists, and horizontal rules help break up simple information and provide visual clues to its structure. Fonts, styles, colors, and special characters help you fine-tune the information. A simple way to group style information on a site is the use of HTML styles.

Sample Questions

1. If you have applied center justification to a paragraph and no longer want it, what's the best way to remove it?
   A. Click Left Justify
   B. Click Center Justify
   C. Change the paragraph format
   D. Delete the Font settings

2. In what tag is text color information stored?
   A. `<a>`
   B. `<font>`
   C. `<color>`
   D. `<p>`

3. Where are HTML Styles panel settings stored?
   A. menus.xml
   B. html.xml
   C. fonts.xml
   D. styles.xml

CHAPTER 9

Using Graphics and Rich Media

Introduction

The earliest Web browsers could render only text, and surfing the Web (for the little content that was there) was a decidedly monotonous affair. With the release of Mosaic, the first GUI browser, images could be embedded in HTML pages, and the Web as we now know it—a vast network of rich documents—was born. These days, with advanced browser capabilities and an array of plug-in applications, Web pages can contain animations, video, and sound, but graphics are still by far the most common form of nontextual content.

Graphics are embedded using the `<img>` tag:

```
<img src="button1.gif">
```

Graphics cannot be created using Macromedia Dreamweaver. You use an image editor such as Fireworks to create or modify graphics and then use Dreamweaver to embed the graphics in HTML pages.

In this chapter, we look at the different image formats supported by browsers; you learn how to insert and modify images using Dreamweaver, create image maps, and slice images.

Image Types and Uses

In principle, the `src` attribute of the `<img>` tag can point to any file, but only three image formats are supported by browsers: GIF, JPEG, and PNG. Each of these file formats has its strengths and weaknesses, and optimum page performance and image quality often depend on choosing the appropriate image format for a particular graphic.

Each of these image formats generates bitmapped images, meaning that the data for the image consists of properties for each pixel in a rectangular grid. Vector-based graphics, which instead use mathematical expressions to define regions of an image, can also be used on Web pages, but they require a plug-in application, such as the Flash Player. The differences between the GIF, JPEG, and PNG formats lie in the properties that can be defined in the data and methods that are used to reduce the file size.

Minimizing the size of graphics files is often an issue in the choice of format because image data in general is large compared to text data and often makes up the bulk of page weight—a large factor in the time it takes for a page (meaning here the HTML file and all dependent files) to be downloaded to the client system. Each image format has a vehicle for reducing file size, but the mechanisms are different and affect the quality of the image in different ways.

GIFs

GIF was the first graphical format supported by browsers and is still probably the most widely used. The limitation of GIFs is that they can contain no more than 256 colors.

GIF file size can be reduced by a method called *bit-depth reduction*, which means limiting the number of colors used in the graphic. The number of colors used can be specified as 2 raised to any power from 1 to 8—in other words, 2, 4, 8, 16, 32, 64, 128, or 256 colors. Bit-depth reduction is called a lossless compression method because aside from the number of colors, no data for the image is lost. This means that shapes, lines, shading, and other image properties are unaffected by reducing the bit depth.

Given these properties, GIF is generally the preferred format for graphics created on a computer, in contrast to scanned or digital photographs. The exception is graphics that use fine color gradients; the limited number of colors available generally is not adequate for gradients. On the other hand, even photographs that contain a limited number of colors can be saved in GIF format with acceptable results.

Two special forms of GIF images are *transparent* and *animated*.

Transparent GIFS

In transparent GIFs, one of the colors contained in the graphic is declared transparent, and any portion of the image containing that color will be invisible.

Transparent GIFs primarily are used to produce the effect of a nonrectangular image by making the canvas on which figures are superimposed invisible.

Animated GIFs

Animated GIFs contain multiple, ordinary GIFs that are displayed in a specific sequence, like frames of a film. In addition to the order of display, the rate of change and looping specifications for the animation can be specified.

Each image in an animated GIF should have the same height and width.

JPEGs

One advantage that JPEG graphics have over GIFs is that they can contain an unlimited number of colors. On the other hand, the compression method for JPEGs is "lossy," unlike lossless bit-depth reduction method.

Increasing the compression ratio reduces the file size for JPEGs. What this means is that some of the data that defines the properties for the individual pixels is deleted, and the properties are instead interpolated from the values of surrounding pixels. As the compression ratio increases, more and more data defining the graphic is lost, and all aspects of the image are affected. How much compression can be used without affecting the image quality in unacceptable ways varies according to the nature of the graphic. Increasing the compression ratio is irreversible—after the data has been deleted, it cannot be restored to the image.

The JPEG format is generally best for scanned or digital photographs or for graphics containing fine color gradients.

PNGs

The PNG format combines the strengths of the GIF and JPEG formats, allowing an unlimited number of colors while supporting bit-depth reduction for compression.

Unfortunately, the PNG format came much later and enjoys limited browser support. Internet Explorer has supported it for several years, but Netscape introduced native PNG support only with version 6.0; a plug-in is available for earlier versions.

Inserting Images

Dreamweaver provides several ways to insert images into pages:

- Insert menu—Insert, Image.
- Objects panel—Common objects group.
- Assets panel—Drag images into the document or select an image and click the Insert button.
- Site window—Drag images into the document or use the Point-to-File tool in the Property Inspector. (This tool appears only in the context of an `<img>` tag; therefore, it is more useful for changing image source files than for inserting images.)

Image Properties

A number of important attributes exist for the `<img>` tag. These are exposed by the Dreamweaver Property Inspector. If you instead want to use CSS properties to manage the display properties, you can define a style rule for the `<img>` or use a class or ID rule for properties that are particular to some images. Here we will look at the HTML attributes for the `<img>` tag only.

Table 9.1 Image Properties

Property	Description
W (width)	Width of the image in pixels; can be any value but is generally the actual width of the graphic.
H (height)	Height of the image in pixels; can be any value but is generally the actual height of the graphic.
SRC	A full or partial URL for the graphical file that provides the image source; relative paths may be from the current document or the Web document root.
Link	Full or partial URL for a hyperlink attached to the image (created by an anchor tag rather than an attribute of the `<img>` tag).
Align	For right or left values, aligns the image along the specified margin of the page, allowing content that follows to flow around the image; other values are for inline images and position the image vertically, relative to the text baseline.
Target	Target frame for linked pages.
Alt	Provides alternative text in case the image is not displayed; it is important to provide alt text as required by accessibility guidelines.
Vspace	Vertical whitespace that will appear around the displayed image.
Hspace	Horizontal whitespace that will appear around the displayed image.
Low Src	A full or partial URL for the graphical file that provides the image source.
Border	Border around the image in pixels (the text color for the page is used, or the link color if the image is a link); many browsers have a default value for the border, so to suppress the image border, you should explicitly set the value to `0`.

TIP

You should always use the height and width properties because this enables the browser to set aside the required space for the image even before it has been downloaded. Reducing the height and width properties is not an appropriate way to create thumbnail versions of images; these properties are not related to the size of the file that must be downloaded to display the image. A legitimate use exists for embedding an image with the height and width each set to 1—the minimum value allowed—on a page users are likely to view before they view the page where the image is actually used as content. This allows the image to be cached on the client system before it is needed in a page. Images embedded with height and width set to 1 for caching purposes should be placed at the very end of the body so as not to slow the loading of other page content.

The HTML code for an image will look something like the following:

```
<img
src="diver.jpg"
width="229"
height="233"
lowsrc="scuba.jpg"
alt="Scuba Diver and Reefs"
align="left"
vspace="5"
hspace="5"
border="1">
```

The Property Inspector provides some additional tools for creating image maps (covered in the next section), for aligning the image using a `<div>` tag, and for editing the image.

The Edit button opens the image for editing in the editor defined for images in the Dreamweaver preferences. If you use Fireworks as your image editor, some additional integration features are available:

- Source file editing—If the image was exported from a PNG file created in Fireworks, you can edit the PNG file instead, and the GIF or JPEG file will be re-exported automatically when you are finished.
- Associated HTML code editing—If the image is associated with HTML code generated by Fireworks, you can choose to edit the code along with the image. Fireworks automatically regenerates the HTML code when you are finished editing the image.
- Round-trip editing—When you are finished editing the image, Fireworks does whatever is necessary to update the page in Dreamweaver.

If you modify the height and width of an image while you edit it or change the height and width properties without modifying the image itself, you can use the Reset Size button to set the properties to the correct values.

Image Maps

Dreamweaver makes the tedious job of creating image maps easy by allowing you to draw areas over parts of an image and create links from them.

To create an image map, you must first embed the image in the document. Then, in the Property Inspector, you enter a name for the map into the Map field. The map is now defined and requires defined areas and links to which they correspond.

To define areas, you click one of the three shape options beneath the Map field in the Property Inspector and then draw the area over a portion of the image. For rectangular and elliptical shapes, you simply click and drag to define the shape. For polygon areas, you click to define successive nodes of the polygon until you have defined the area.

After the areas are defined, you can use the Pointer Hotspot tool in the Property Inspector to select areas and define their properties. You can also modify the position and size of the area as needed.

The code for an image map will look like the following:

```
<img src="menu.gif" width="80" height="200" usemap="#nav" border="0">
<map name="nav">
  <area shape="rect" coords="8,15,74,37" href="form.htm">
  <area shape="circle" coords="38,78,28" href="home.htm">
</map>
```

> **NOTE**
> Fireworks also has excellent image-mapping tools. If you create image maps in Fireworks, you can export the HTML along with the image and import it into Dreamweaver using the Objects panel. The round-trip editing feature enables you to open image maps created in Fireworks from Dreamweaver, and both the HTML and images will be updated automatically when you complete your editing in Fireworks.

Slicing Images

Image slicing is a technique used to improve page performance as an alternative to image maps, and also for large images that are not used as image maps.

Image slicing consists of cutting a large image into several smaller images and then creating a carefully constructed HTML table in which to display the slices so that they appear as a seamless image. You can create hyperlinks from the various slices, just as you would for any image, to create the effect of an image map.

The performance gains attained by image slicing occur because browsers can open several simultaneous connections to the Web server for downloading dependent files. Although a single large image must be downloaded through a single connection, many or all of the smaller slices made from the image can be downloaded at the same time.

> **TIP**
> Note, however, that for small images, opening multiple connections to download the slices may take longer than downloading the single image. Image slices also require more work on the part of the browser to process the multiple `<img>` tags and the code for the table that contains the slices. For large images, image slicing generally produces better page performance for the end user, but for smaller images, performance might be worse for a sliced image.

Image slicing cannot be performed within Dreamweaver itself. An image editor such as Fireworks is required. Fireworks is an ideal choice because it not only has tools to help you slice images, but it also generates the HTML table code, which you export with the image slices and import into Dreamweaver using the Objects panel.

Summary

- Images are embedded in HTML documents using the <img> tag.
- Browsers support as many as three types of images: GIF, JPEG, and PNG. Each has advantages and disadvantages in the compression mechanisms used to reduce file size.
- Image file size is reduced by bit-depth reduction (GIF and PNG), in which only the number of colors used is reduced, or through increasing the compression ratio (JPEG), in which general image data is deleted and interpolated.
- Dreamweaver provides several ways of inserting images into documents.
- Paths to image files, like paths for hyperlinks, may be full URLs or partial URLs with paths relative to the current document or the Web document root.
- Numerous properties for images can be set through the Property Inspector.
- Dreamweaver has image-mapping tools to help you define areas of the image that are hot spots for hyperlinked pages.
- Slicing large images using Fireworks or another graphics editor generally improves performance and provides an alternative way to produce the effect of an image map.

Sample Questions

1. Which properties control the whitespace around images? (Choose two)
   A. `border`
   B. `hspace`
   C. `vspace`
   D. `padding`

2. Which image format is generally best for scanned photographs embedded in Web pages?
   A. GIF
   B. JPEG
   C. PNG
   D. BMP

CHAPTER 10

Linking Pages and Sites

Introduction

Hyperlinks are the heart of the World Wide Web, allowing users to move to any page available on the Web by clicking a "hotspot" that may be attached to a text string or an image. Typically, links point to another HTML page that may be on the same site (in the same physical or virtual directory tree on one server) or another site.

Hyperlinks are created using the anchor (<a>) tag, and the most important attribute is the `href` (hypertext reference), which defines the document to which the link points. Any text or images inside the start and closing anchor tags will be the hotspot. A typical anchor tag might look like this:

```
<a href="http://www.w3.org/TR/html4/sgml/sgmldecl.html">
  SGML Declaration of HTML 4
</a>
```

A link can point to any file that can be accessed through a Web server, however, and not just to other HTML pages. If the browser or one of its registered plug-in programs is capable of displaying the file, it will be opened in the browser or in a window created by the plug-in. If the file cannot be directly displayed, the browser will prompt the user to download it.

> **TIP**
>
> E-mail links can be created by using `mailto:email address` as the `href` value. The browser will prompt the default mail program on the client system or the mail program specified in the browser settings to open a new message window with the specified address in the To field.

Links can also be used to execute JavaScript (provided that the user has not disabled script execution). JavaScript code is executed by setting the anchor tag's `href` (hypertext reference) attribute to `JavaScript: [JavaScript statements]`. The entire script block to be executed may be embedded in the `href` value, or you can invoke a function defined elsewhere.

Text used as a hotspot is generally displayed by browsers in blue (hex code #0000FF) and underlined, by default. If the link has been visited recently (that is, if it appears in the browser's history) the color is changed to purple. An additional change in color or appearance might occur when the link is active. If an image is used for the hotspot and if the image has a border (defined in the `<img>` tag), the border color will follow the same rules as the link color.

> **NOTE**
>
> The colors for links can be overridden using the `link`, `vlink`, and `alink` attributes of the `<body>` tag. More elaborate redefinitions of appearance can be made using cascading style sheets (CSS). In addition to defining a general style rule for the `<a>` tag, you can also define styles for the pseudo-classes `a:link`, `a:visited`, `a:active`, and `a:hover`. If you want to remove the underlining of links, you must do it through CSS (some browsers allow the user to display links with underlining, but as a developer, you have no control over that).

In GUI browsers, the presence of a hotspot is also indicated by a change in the appearance of the mouse pointer. By default, the pointer changes to a pointing hand.

Complete and Partial URLs

When a user clicks a hotspot, the browser sends the `href` value of the anchor tag out to a Web server through the Internet. This means, of course, that the `href` value is a URL, because that is the kind of request Web servers understand. HTML allows the value to take the form of a full or partial URL, however.

A full URL is a complete address for a file accessible through the Internet, such as `http://www.zmag.org/ZNET.htm` or `http://250.78.65.51/index.htm`. If no specific page is specified in the URL, as in `http://www.macromedia.com/`, the Web server will look for a default page in the directory specified. If no default page is found, the server will return an error page or a listing of all files in the directory, if directory browsing is allowed. Default page names and directory browsing permission are set up in the Web server administration.

> **TIP**
>
> Although `http://www.macromedia.com` is a valid `href` value, ending URLs for default pages with a trailing slash (`http://www.macromedia.com/`) will slightly improve performance. Without the ending slash, the URL is technically faulty and must be corrected by the browser.

If the file you are linking to is part of the same site—on the same server—you can also use partial URLs for `href` values. A partial URL omits the domain/IP address information, which is added to the request by the browser.

If the file linked to exists in the same directory as the current page, the filename is adequate for the partial URL:

```
<a href="library.htm">Resources</a>
```

If the file resides in a different directory, the partial URL must also include a relative path to the location of the other file.

Options for Relative Paths

Relative paths may be defined in two ways:

- Relative to the location of the current document
- Relative to the Web document root (which is defined in the Web server administration)

Paths Relative to the Location of the Current Document

Paths relative to the current location are defined using the following syntax:

Table 10.1 Paths Relative to the Current Document Location

Path Fragment	Description
`./`	Current directory
`../`	Up one directory level
`subdirectory/`	Subdirectory

You can define a path up and down as many directory levels as you like, or you can go up one or more directory levels and then down a different path of subdirectories from that point.

For example, the following path locates a file called `index.html` that is located in a subdirectory called `tech` of the directory `resources`, which is a subdirectory of the current directory:

```
href="resources/tech/index.html"
```

Following is another example, mapping a path up two levels from the current location and then down through two subdirectories:

```
href="../../products/widgets/index.html"
```

Paths Relative to the Web Document Root

Paths relative to the Web document root begin with a forward slash (signifying the Web document root directory itself) followed by subdirectories:

```
href="/mysite/products/index.html"
```

Choosing the Pathing Method in Macromedia Dreamweaver

General options for creating links in Macromedia Dreamweaver are covered later in this chapter. Here we will look only at setting the pathing option in Dreamweaver.

By default, Dreamweaver creates paths relative to the current document. To use paths relative to the Web document root, you must first define a site. You can then place the cursor inside a link hotspot and select Modify, Change Link. In the Select File dialog box that opens, you can change the Relative To field from Document to Site Root.

> **CAUTION**
>
> The slightly misleading terminology "site root" in the Select File is instructive. Dreamweaver assumes that the site root is identical to the Web document root and writes the path accordingly. There is no way to define the Web document root explicitly, so if you want Dreamweaver to automatically create paths relative to the Web document root, you must define the site so that the site root is the Web document root.
>
> Also, note that after you change a link to Web Document Root Relative, Dreamweaver assumes that you want to create all future links in the same way. To force Dreamweaver to create paths relative to the current document again, change a link to Document Relative.

What Pathing Method to Use

Both relative pathing methods have advantages and disadvantages.

If you use paths relative to the current document, the site will be entirely portable, meaning that the links do not depend on where the site root is located relative to the Web document root. You could change the physical or virtual file structure so that `[web document root]/mysite/` becomes `[web document root]/sites/mysite/`, and the links would be unaffected. On the other hand, if you move a file within the site file system—`mysite/products.html` becomes `mysite/products/products.html`, for example—all links to and from that page will be broken.

The advantage of links relative to the Web document root is that the path is written the same way regardless of where you are linking. For example, `href="/mysite/index.html"` works whether the page that contains the anchor tag is in `/mysite/products/` or `/mysite/services/training/`. Also, if you move the page within the site, links to the page will be broken because its relation to the Web document root will change, but links contained in the page will be unaffected.

Which you should use depends on several factors:

- If you create a site definition for your site in Dreamweaver, the site-management tools will take care of automatically updating links when you move files, so which pathing method you use does not really matter.
- If the site is large and files are added and moved frequently (the two factors usually go hand in hand), using Dreamweaver's site management may not be

practical, and paths relative to the Web document root will probably be easier to create and maintain.

- If you dynamically generate links through some kind of server-side processing, paths relative to the Web document root will be simpler to use.
- If you have no control over the overall file structure on the server (beyond your own site) and the structure is subject to change, paths relative to the current document location are less vulnerable to link breakage.

Using Named Anchors

Named anchors work like bookmarks in pages: they produce no visible change in the content but provide a hidden place marker that a link elsewhere can point to. Named targets are created by adding the name attribute to an anchor tag, which may or may not also have an `href` value to provide a link to another location:

```
<a name="top"></a>
```

or

```
<a href="#top" name="section1">Back to the top</a>
```

The second example in the preceding code also shows how links point to a named anchor. The # sign in front of the name indicates a named anchor. If the `href` value contains only an anchor name, as in this example, the named anchor must be in the same page. A link can also point to another page with a named anchor appended to the filename to open the new page at the point of the anchor rather than the top of the page:

```
<a href="article1002.htm#section1"
```

> **NOTE**
>
> Note that the anchor name is case sensitive when it is referenced in an `href` value.

Named anchors are created in Dreamweaver using the Insert menu or the Invisibles category in the Objects panel.

Targeting Links

The target attribute of the anchor tag is generally used with pages in framesets to specify which frame the linked page should open in:

```
<a href="products.htm" target="mainFrame">Products</a>
```

The value for the target in this case must be a name specified using the name attribute of the `<frame>` tag. If the frame named in the target value does not exist, the new page will open in the current frame or browser window.

The target also has four special predefined values, which all begin with the underscore (_) character:

Table 10.2 Predefined Target Values

Value	Description
`_self`	Opens the new page in the current frame (because this is the default value, there is rarely, if ever, a need to specify it).
`_parent`	Opens the new page in the parent frame of the current frame that is part of a nested frameset, thus eliminating the nested frameset (if the current frameset is not nested, this `_parent` is equivalent to `_top`).
`_top`	Opens the new page in the full browser window, thus removing all framesets.
`_blank`	Opens the new page in a new, separate browser window, without closing the current window; the new window will have the same size and features as the current one.

NOTE

Note that all values for the target, whether predefined or the name of an existing frame, are case sensitive.

TIP

Using the JavaScript `window.open()` method instead of targeting a link to `_blank` allows you to specify the size and position of the new window, as well as what features it has, such as toolbars, an address bar, scroll bars, and so on. You can also control the new window from the window that opened it, and vice versa, using JavaScript, which you cannot do with a window opened using the `_blank` target.

Creating Links Using Dreamweaver

You can create links in Dreamweaver in several ways. Which way is most convenient partly depends on your editing style and partly on the kind of link you are creating.

Creating Full URL Links

To create a link using a full URL, you can select the text or image for the hotspot and type or paste the address into the Link field in the Property Inspector. Full URLs used for links are also tracked and cataloged for your site in the URL category of the site Assets, and you can enter a previously used URL into the Link field from the Assets panel.

If the URL changes, you can change the `href` value in all links by using the Change Link Sitewide command, which is available in the Site window.

Creating Partial URL Links

Partial URL links can be created using the Site Map in the Site window or using the Property Inspector for an open page.

Using the Site Map to Create Partial URL Links

You can select files in the Site Map and create links to new or existing files using the right-click menu (Link to New File or Link to Existing File options). To link to existing files, you can also use the Point-to-File crosshairs.

Creating links through the Site Map is of limited use, mainly for creating new navigation pages or defining basic linkage in a new site, because the links are created using the filename (without the extension) and inserted at the end of the page body.

> **CAUTION**
>
> This method does not work for pages created from templates, unless the page has been detached from the template.

Using the Property Inspector to Create Partial URL Links

For any selected text or image, the Property Inspector will display a Link field where you can type in a full or partial URL, including named anchors, or a `mailto:` link. Beside the link field is a Point-to-File crosshairs icon, which you can click and drag over a file in the Site window to create a partial URL link. You can also click a folder icon to browse for and select a file to create the link.

You can also drag the Point-to-File crosshairs over a named anchor icon in the current or any other open page to create a link to the named anchor.

Creating `Mailto:` Links

You can type `mailto:` links into the Link field in the Property Inspector, as explained in the previous section. You can also create `mailto:` links using the Insert menu or the Common category of the Objects panel.

Updating Links

When you move files using the Site window, Dreamweaver will prompt you to automatically update all affected links. Full URL and `mailto:` links are not updated, because they are not affected by changing the location of the page.

Summary

Links are created using the anchor (`<a>`) tag. The appearance of hotspots indicating links in a page is defined by attributes of the `<body>` tag or CSS rules. The `href` attribute of the `<a>` tag defines the location of a page or file linked to using a full or partial URL, with or without named anchors. E-mail links are also created using the `href` value `mailto:email address`. Paths for partial URLs can be defined relative to the Web document root or the location of the current page.

Named anchors are created using the name attribute of the `<a>` tag and are referenced in `href` values by the name preceded by a # sign.

The target attribute of the `<a>` tag causes the linked page to open in a specific frame of a frameset or a new browser window.

Dreamweaver provides several ways of inserting images into documents and automatically updates links when you move files using the Site window.

Sample Questions

1. Which of the following tags in the page article.htm will successfully link to a named anchor in the same page defined by the following code:
   <a name="section1"></a>

   A. <a href="_section1">Section 1</a>
   B. <a href="#section1">Section 1</a>
   C. <a href="#Section1">Section 1</a>
   D. <a anchor="section1">Section 1</a>

2. Which of the following links will open a new browser window? (Choose 2)

   A. <a href="index.htm" target="_new">Index</a>
   B. <a href="index.htm" target="_blank">Index</a>
   C. <a href="index.htm" target="window.open()">Index</a>
   D. <a href="JavaScript:window.open('index.htm','newWin')">Index</a>

CHAPTER 11

Importing External Content

Macromedia Dreamweaver enables you to import data from other sources, such as tabular data from a spreadsheet or a database table. It also enables you to clean up the HTML that is generated by Microsoft Word so that it is usable on the Web. Even XML content can be imported into Dreamweaver, thus giving you the capability to use content easily from various sources in your Web pages.

Importing Tabular Data

You can easily copy the text from a spreadsheet and paste it into Dreamweaver; however, it formats the data using only page breaks, or it uses no formatting at all.

Dreamweaver can import data that is saved into a delimited format from a spreadsheet and can format the data into an HTML table. Delimiters (separators) between each data value can be tab characters, commas, colons, semicolons, or any other delimiter. Each row in the file must have the same number of fields separated by a delimiter. The following example shows data that is delimited by the use of a comma:

```
1011,Bob Jones,bjones@anywhere.com
1012,Ted Baker,tbaker@mysite.com
1013,Mary Shields,mary_shields@fsl.com
```

Microsoft Excel enables you to save spreadsheets delimited by commas or tabs. Most databases also allow you to export your table data into delimited format. All these sources can be imported into Dreamweaver as long as the data is formatted correctly.

> **NOTE**
> Comma-delimited files are commonly stored with a .csv extension.

Dreamweaver will automatically format the imported tabular data into an HTML table.

Use the File, Import, Import Tabular Data menu item to specify the file to import, as well as the information listed in Table 11.1:

Table 11.1 Import Tabular Data Dialog Options

Setting	Description
Data File	Browse to a delimited file.
Delimiter	Specify the delimiter of the data.
Table Width	Select Fit to Data to create a table that adjusts to the longest text string in each table column. Select Set to specify a table width as a percentage of the browser window or as a number of pixels.
Cell Padding	Set the space between the data and the table cell.
Cell Spacing	Set the space between the table cells.
Format Top Row	Add bold and/or italic to the table header.
Border	Specify the width of the border around the table cells.

Exporting Tabular Data

You can also export an HTML table from Dreamweaver into a delimited file. This delimited file can easily be imported back into spreadsheets, databases, and other applications that enable delimited sources of data.

Export the table by selecting the table or locating your cursor anywhere inside a table cell. Choose File, Export, Export Table. The resulting dialog box enables you to specify the delimiter as well as the format for the line breaks, whether for Unix, Mac, or Windows.

Importing Word HTML

You can't directly import a Microsoft Word document into Dreamweaver. If you want to import the contents of a Word file, you must first save the file as HTML and then import the file into Dreamweaver.

Use the File, Import, Import Word HTML dialog box to specify the resulting HTML file to import. After you choose a file, you will be prompted to clean up the resulting HTML.

Cleaning Up Microsoft Word HTML

Microsoft Word puts in HTML that is used within Word and is not necessary or desirable in pages on the Web. Dreamweaver cleans up Word HTML either on demand or when you try to import a file that is detected as having been saved by Word. This feature works on files created by Word 97 or later.

> **CAUTION**
>
> The process of cleaning the document may render the file unusable to Word. Therefore, you should save a backup copy of the file before cleaning up the HTML.

You can import Word HTML using File, Import, Import Word HTML.

When you receive the Clean Up Word dialog box, you will be asked to set options for cleaning. Basic options are described in Table 11.2.

Table 11.2 Clean Up Word HTML Basic Options

Setting	Description
Remove All Word-Specific Markup	Removes all Word-specific HTML. Each option can be selected individually from the Detailed tab.
Clean Up CSS	Removes all Word-specific CSS. Further customize these options using the Detailed tab.
Clean Up `<font>` Tags Tags (Clean Up Word dialog box)>	Removes `<font>` tags, converting the default body text to size 2 HTML text.
Fix Invalidly Nested Tags	Removes the font markup tags inserted by Word outside the paragraph and heading (block-level) tags.
Set Background Color	Allows you to enter a hexadecimal value to set the background color of your document. The Word HTML document defaults to gray. The default hexadecimal value set by Dreamweaver is white.
Apply Source Formatting	Applies the source formatting options you specify in HTML Format preferences and SourceFormat.txt to the document.
Show Log on Completion	Displays an alert box with details about the changes made to the document as soon as the cleanup is finished.

> **TIP**
>
> The SourceFormat.txt file (in the Dreamweaver/Configuration folder) provides precise specifications for formatting code. You can edit this file in any text editor and control exactly how Dreamweaver writes code. You can change certain tag-specific options in this file that you can't change using the Code Format preferences.

If Dreamweaver is unable to determine the version of Word, select the correct version using the pop-up menu.

Working with XML Content

Dreamweaver enables you to import and export content that is formatted as XML. XML is the eXtensible Markup Language, a markup language for structured documents.

XML uses block tags (opening and closing tags) to describe the contents of the data inside. One difference between XML and HTML is that each tag is required to be closed. Tags such as the `<IMG>` tag, which does not have a closing tag in HTML, must use a closing slash before the closing angle bracket.

```
<img src="sunny.gif" />
```

Exporting a page to XML will ensure that all tags live up to XML's more strict syntax.

If you have documents that are based on templates with editable regions, Dreamweaver allows you to export those pages in XML syntax so that other programs can work on the data, such as XML parsers. Conversely, if you have an XML document that's structured appropriately, you can import the data from it into a document based on a Dreamweaver template.

Exporting XML Content

To export a file to XML syntax, open a file that is based on a template (has editable regions). Select File, Export, Export Editable Regions as XML. Dreamweaver will prompt you to choose a tag notation.

You can choose from two types of XML tag notations: editable region name tags or standard Dreamweaver XML tags. Choose the notation that best suits how XML content is incorporated into your Web site.

Dreamweaver generates an XML file containing the material from the document's editable regions. The XML file includes the name of the template the document is based on, as well as the name and contents of each editable region. Material in the locked regions is not exported to the XML file.

Importing XML Content

Select File, Import, Import XML into Template to import an XML file. Dreamweaver creates a new document based on the template specified in the XML file. It then fills in the contents of each editable region in that document using the data in the XML file. The resulting document appears in a new Document window. If the specified template is not found, Dreamweaver prompts you to select a template to use.

> **NOTE**
>
> If your XML file isn't set up exactly the way Dreamweaver expects, you may not be able to import your data. Export an XML file from Dreamweaver and then copy the data from the original XML file into this file to ensure the correct format.

> **NOTE**
>
> Don't confuse importing XML content with a truly dynamic Web page. After it is imported, this information remains static. Changes would require you to remove the content and import another XML document.

Summary

Dreamweaver enables you to import data from a delimited file and then formats it in tabular format automatically. These delimited files can easily be created by spreadsheet, word processing, and in most cases, database applications.

Microsoft Word creates HTML tags that are only usable internally and that are not necessary or desirable within Web pages. Dreamweaver enables you to import and clean up Word HTML documents quickly and easily.

Dreamweaver also enables you to export and import XML data to and from your templatized Web pages. The data on these XML pages can then be edited from within other applications, such as XML parsers.

Sample Questions

1. How can you import information and have it automatically formatted into an HTML table?
   A. Copy and paste from a spreadsheet
   B. Import a delimited file
   C. Copy and paste from a word processing document
   D. Import an XML document

2. What types of tags does Dreamweaver not clean from Microsoft Word documents when prompted?
   A. XML from HTML tags
   B. All CSS tags
   C. <font> tags
   D. Invalid nesting of tags

CHAPTER 12

Adding Interactivity Using Forms

HTML forms are the primary mechanism for receiving user input on the Web. For example, you can use forms to create search interfaces, provide input interfaces for customer information, or collect survey information.

Creating Forms

An HTML form consists of a container `<form>` tag with form objects within it that accept user input and allow the user to submit the form.

To create a form and form objects, use the Forms Object panel or the Insert menu. Start by creating the form itself, which accepts the following three attributes:

- Form Name
- Action
- Method

Form Name

Each form can be created with a unique name. This name is used only to reference the form when using a scripting language, such as JavaScript. JavaScript can be used to validate user input into the form objects. Input this name in the Property Inspector for the form tag.

Action

HTML provides a mechanism for prompting for user input. A form's submitted data can be processed using a programming or scripting language. This page or script is designated in the action setting of the form Property Inspector.

If the form data were submitted to a CGI script, the URL would be formed as in the sample URL that follows:

```
http://www.site.com/cgi-bin/register.cgi
```

In this case, the `register.cgi` script would process the submitted form data.

You may also specify a `mailto:` URL for the action value. Depending on your browser and version, this setting will turn all form values into a document for attachment to an e-mail message.

Method

The method of the form indicates the way in which the form data will be sent to the action page. The method has two values: `GET` and `POST`. The default value of `GET` will pass all user-input values to the action page by appending them to the end of the URL. The value `POST` will send the form values in the body of the message, thus hiding them from the user.

URLs are limited in the number of characters they can hold. Therefore, if the amount of data the user inputs exceeds the allowable URL length, the data will be truncated, and improper results may occur. Additionally, `GET` data is displayed on the URL so any user can see all form data—even hidden information not intended for viewing.

Creating a form using Dreamweaver results in the creation of the HTML `<form>` tag. An example of a resulting tag is shown next:

```
<form name="register" method="post"
action="http://www.site.com/cgi-bin/register.cgi">

</form>
```

Form Objects

After you have created the container `<form>` tag, you can insert form objects inside this tag using the Forms Object panel or the Insert menu. Form objects are the user-interface elements that accept user data. Several types of form objects, their usage, and their description are discussed next:

- Textual Input Fields
- Buttons
- Check Box
- Radio Button
- List/Menu
- File fields
- Hidden fields

In addition to these form objects, the Forms Object panel also allows you to insert an image and enables you to create a JavaScript jump menu.

Textual Input Fields

Three types of text fields are enabled in forms: text, password, and text area.

A text object takes a number of characters in a single line edit box. The only limitation on the number of characters is where specified or as limited by the browser. Control characters are not allowed in text fields.

Password objects are similar to text objects, except that they mask the input with asterisks (*). This type of text object is used for passwords and other sensitive information. Note, however, that it only masks the input that the user sees—it does not encrypt the data that is sent to the server.

Text area objects are long, unlimited text fields used for comments, notes, and other long text fields. These types of objects can accept control characters.

Attributes of the textual input fields are listed in Table 12.1:

Table 12.1 Text Object Attributes

Attribute	Description
`TextField`	Unique name of the text object on the form. Used to reference the object using a scripting language, such as JavaScript.
`Char Width`	Visual width of the text object.
`Type`	Specified as Single Line by default, but can be changed either to multiline or password.
`Max Chars`	The maximum number of characters allowed to be input. Used for text and password objects.
`Num Lines`	The size of the text box in the number of lines displayed. Used only for text area objects.
`Init Val`	Initial value the user will see in the object.
`Wrap`	For text area objects, whether the browser will wrap the text with control characters or only for display purposes.

Creating either a text or password field results in the creation of an HTML `<input>` tag. Text area controls are created using a `<textarea>` HTML tag. Examples of these three tags are shown here:

```
<input type="text" name="login">
<input type="password" name="userpass">
<textarea name="comments" rows="5"
       wrap="VIRTUAL">Enter comments here
</textarea>
```

Buttons

Each form must have at least one Submit button. Buttons are the way that users can submit the input data. Other types of buttons enable the form to be reset to the original state and to perform other processing tasks or scripts.

Attributes of buttons are listed in Table 12.2:

Table 12.2 Button Object Attributes

Attribute	Description
`Button Name`	Unique name of the button object on the form. Used to reference the object using a scripting language, such as JavaScript.
`Label`	Text displayed on the button.
`Action`	Determines the action that occurs when the button is clicked. Values are `submit`, `reset`, or `nothing`.

Creating a Submit button creates an `<input>` tag, as shown next:

```
<input type="submit" name="Submit" value="Submit">
```

Check Boxes

A check box can be used alone to allow a user to indicate a yes (checked) or no (unchecked) value. Used in groups, check boxes can formulate multiple-choice responses, such as those used for test or survey questions.

Attributes for check boxes are shown in Table 12.3:

Table 12.3 Check Box Object Attributes

Attribute	Description
`CheckBox Name`	Unique name of the check box object on the form. Used to reference the object using a scripting language, such as JavaScript.
`Checked Value`	Value sent to the action page or script on submission if the check box is checked.
`Initial State`	Choose either Checked or Unchecked to determine the initial state of the check box.

Check boxes are created using the HTML `<input>` tag, as shown here:

```
<input type="checkbox" name="newsletter" value="checkbox">
```

Radio Buttons

Radio buttons enable only one selection from two or more choices. Grouping radio buttons is accomplished by giving each member of the group the same name attribute.

> **TIP**
>
> Radio buttons are most effective when used in groups of three to five options. If you have more options, you should probably use a list/menu object to save on browser window space.

Attributes of radio buttons are listed in Table 12.4:

Table 12.4 Radio Button Object Attributes

Attribute	Description
`RadioButton`	Unique name of the radio button object on the form, used as a group. Used to reference the object using a scripting language, such as JavaScript.
`Checked Value`	Value sent to the action page or script on submission if the radio button is chosen.
`Initial State`	Choose either Checked or Unchecked to determine the initial state of the radio button. Set only one radio button to checked within the group.

Each radio button is created using the HTML `<input>` tag, as shown next:

```
<input type="radio" name="frequency" value="daily">
```

List/Menu Objects

List and menu objects enable selection from a drop-down list of options.

Menu objects enable the selection of only one choice, and only one value is displayed until the user clicks the down area and expands the object to see the rest.

For multiple selections, a list object displays several options and allows scrolling for additional options. Users can make multiple selections from the list.

Table 12.5 List/Menu Object Attributes

Attribute	Description
`List/Menu`	Unique name of the list/menu object on the form. Used to reference the object using a scripting language, such as JavaScript.
`Type`	Either Menu or List.
`Height`	When the type is set to List, specifies how many options are displayed before expanding.
`Selections Allow Multiple`	When the type is set to List, indicates that multiple selections are allowed.
`List Values`	Displays the List Values dialog box in which multiple options may be entered.
`Initially Selected`	Specifies the list values that will be selected when the form loads; corresponds to the list values entered.

List/menu objects are created using the `<select>` tag, with each list or menu item listed in an `<option>` tag. An example of a list/menu control follows:

```
<select name="age">
        <option value="young" selected>20-34</option>
        <option value="middle">35-49</option>
        <option value="senior">50+</option>
</select>
<input type="radio" name="frequency" value="daily">
```

File Field Objects

File Field objects enable uploading from a client file to the Web server. This object has two parts: a text box for the filename and a Browse button to enable local file system exploring (see Table 12.6).

Table 12.6 File Object Attributes

Attribute	Description
`FileField Name`	Unique name of the file object on the form. Used to reference the object using a scripting language, such as JavaScript.
`Char Width`	Visual width of the text object.
`Max Chars`	The maximum number of characters allowed to be input.

To use a file object, the form `Method` must be set to `POST`. The file would need to be uploaded by a scripting or application program on the action page.

> **NOTE**
> Confirm that anonymous file uploads are allowed before using the file field. If you insert a file object with Macromedia Dreamweaver, an additional attribute will be put into the form tag (*ENCTYPE=*`"multipart/form-data"`) to ensure that the file is encoded properly.

File controls are created using the HTML `<input>`, as shown next:

```
<input type="file" name="UploadFile" size="50" maxlength="100">
```

Hidden Fields

Hidden fields enable data to be passed from the form to the action page without the user seeing them. This type of control is most often used for programmatic reasons and behind-the-scenes processing.

The only attributes of a hidden form object are a unique `name` and a `value` to be passed.

Hidden form fields are created using an `<input>` tag with a `type` of `hidden`, as shown next:

```
<input type="hidden" name="UserID">
```

Form Value Validation

When prompting for user data, it is often desirable or necessary to check the user input for validity. You can require that an entry be input or selected in a form or verify that the input text value is in a valid format using form validation.

To validate the data input into a form, you use a Dreamweaver behavior. These behaviors can be attached to forms and form objects using the Behaviors panel when that form or object is selected. Two types of form validation are

- Validate Form
- Set Text of Text Field

Use of these behaviors generates and inserts JavaScript code into the page.

Validate Form

The Validate Form behavior checks the contents of the specified text object to ensure that the user has entered the correct type of data. This behavior is available only if a text object has been inserted into the document. When attaching the Validate Form behavior to a form object, you must specify which text object is to be validated. Each form object must have a unique name, and that unique name is chosen for validation.

CAUTION

If you use the same name for two objects, behaviors may not work properly—even if the objects are in different forms.

Attach a behavior using of the following methods:

- To validate individual fields as the user fills out the form, select a text field and choose Window, Behaviors.
- To validate multiple fields when the user submits the form, click the `<form>` tag in the Tag Selector in the bottom-left corner of the Document window and choose Window, Behaviors.

Choose Validate Form from the Actions pop-up menu. Choose the field or fields you want to validate. You can specify that data input is required and accept data in any of the following formats:

- Use Anything
- E-mail Address
- Number
- Number From (within a range of numbers)

Attach this action to individual text fields with the `onBlur` event to validate the fields as the user is filling out the form, or attach it to the form with the `onSubmit` event to evaluate several text fields at once when the user clicks the Submit button. Attaching this action to a form prevents the form from being submitted to the server if any of the specified fields contains invalid data.

Set Text of Text Field

The Set Text of Text Field action replaces the content of a form's text field with the content you specify.

You can embed any valid JavaScript function call, property, global variable, or other expression in the text. To embed a JavaScript expression, place it inside braces ({}). To display a brace, precede it with a backslash (\{).

To insert this action, select a text field and open the Behaviors panel. From the Actions pop-up menu, choose Set Text, Set Text of Text Field. Apply this action to the desired text field and choose the desired event.

Summary

Dreamweaver enables you to create HTML forms for prompting for user input. Each form is made up of a set of form objects—text inputs, check boxes, and radio buttons, among others. This data is collected and sent to the page or script specified in the `action` attribute of the `<form>` tag.

Data can be validated through the generation of JavaScript using Dreamweaver built-in behaviors.

Sample Questions

1. Which attribute of a `<form>` tag enables processing of form data?
   A. `Method`
   B. `Action`
   C. `Name`
   D. `Process`
2. Which of the following represent the method of the form? Choose two.
   A. `GET`
   B. `PUT`
   C. `POST`
   D. `RETRIEVE`

CHAPTER 13

Partitioning Interfaces Using Frames

About Frames

Typical HTML documents define what is to be displayed within 100% of the area within a browser window. For various reasons, it is sometimes necessary to divide a browser window into parts, each of which is to display different information to the user. Sometimes this is done with the help of tables, which allow layout to be done in a single HTML document. At other times it is necessary, or even desirable, to break up the page into frames.

Frames allow the developer to slice the browser window into either columns, rows, or a combination of both. Unlike tables, the content of each of the frames is held in its own file. The layout of each frame within the browser window is held in what is called a *frameset*. The frameset is not seen inside the browser window but defines the placement and source file of each of the frames.

Advantages of Frames

Some of the advantages of frames are the following:

- Frames offer a more advanced way of organizing information within a browser window. Each frame is driven by a separate HTML object that can have its own page properties, JavaScript, and CSS settings.
- Frames enable you to build an interface in which only part of the browser window scrolls. This enables you to build navigation that is always onscreen, no matter how long your content is.

- Frames refresh only when they are being updated. This enables your users to always have the navigation of your site available to them, even between page loads and server-side processing.
- Frames can be a simple way of centralizing your navigation into a single file. Building your navigation into a single frame enables you to update only a single file when the structure of your site changes.
- Files do not have to exist in the same directory or server. The frameset and the pages they call can be placed in directories more related to what they do and also can exist on different servers. This enables you to link to pages (or even post form information) from one server to another while maintaining a single interface.
- Frames can be used to store information in the client's browser between pages. Because each frame has its own page environment and only refreshes when it is told to, hidden frames are sometimes used to hold information from page to page within a site.

Disadvantages of Frames

Some disadvantages of frames are the following:

- Although frames can be used safely if your target audience is using modern browsers on common workstations, frames support is not always complete in older browsers and in newer handheld devices, such as PDAs. Also, not all Internet users with disabilities have devices that can successfully interpret and navigate frames.
- Another problem with older browsers and frames is that pre-4.0 browsers do not record the state of all frames within a frameset; they record only a link to the frameset itself, which points users back to the default pages rather than the pages they were viewing when they bookmarked the page.
- Creating links to content pages within frames can also be troublesome because the default content, not necessarily the desired content, will come up when linking to a frameset. Several solutions to this involve either JavaScript or server-side languages, but these take time and effort to implement and manage.
- Compared to other layout tools, such as tables, frames can be difficult to hand code. Fortunately, Dreamweaver takes care of a lot of the issues in creating frames, but the developer must still maintain proper use of targeting when linking between frames and must be aware of frames when doing testing on a site.

Frames Alternatives

Because of the hazards of using frames, many developers shy away from using them. As a substitute, Dreamweaver provides several tools for reusing content across your pages, which is the most common reason for using frames in the first place. Covered in different chapters, they are the following:

Templates

Templates enable you to define what should stay the same from page to page and what should differ. Dreamweaver then enables you to update all the common areas, usually navigation, across all pages.

→ See Chapter 17, "Using Templates," for more information.

Library Items

Library items enable you to create reusable site objects for holding whatever content you need them to hold. Simple update tools allow you to synchronize an entire site in a few clicks.

→ See Chapter 16, "Libraries and Extensions," for more information.

Server-side Includes

Server-side includes enable you to store separate HTML objects on a server and to give the server directions on how to piece them together when an affected page is requested.

→ See Chapter 18, "Server-side Includes," for more information.

About Framesets

Framesets are the pieces of code that divide the browser into frames and give each frame its properties. Framesets appear in a document separate from any of the frames themselves and are visually hidden from the end user. The only content that a normal user will see from a frameset file is the contents of the `<title>` tag, which will appear in the title bar of the browser, if it is showing.

> **NOTE**
> `<title>` tags found in the frame pages are never seen by the user. The `<title>` from the frameset is always used.

Framesets are loaded into a browser by clicking a link that leads to the document or by typing in the URL for the document. Framesets do not need to be specified or loaded in any special way.

Framesets can divide the browser window into columns, rows, or both columns and rows. The frameset contains information for each resulting frame. Unlike tables, a frameset cannot be used to partially divide a browser into columns or rows. No spanning or joining of frames is allowed. If the desired interface calls for frames spanned or cut to make irregular shapes, nested frames must be used.

Frameset and Frame Source Code

A simple frameset, for instance, could break up the browser window into a left navigation area and leave the remainder of the browser window for content. This would look like the following:

```
<html>
<head>
   <title>My Site</title>
</head>

<frameset cols="80,*">
   <frame name="nav" src="navigation.htm">
   <frame name="content" src="home.htm">
</frameset>
</html>
```

The first thing that is apparent is the lack of a `<body>` tag. Because the frameset itself does not contain any content (that's left for the pages in each frame), the frameset does not need a `<body>` tag. Instead, a `<frameset>` tag is used to let the browser know that the document plans on dividing the browser window into frames.

The next thing to notice is that even though the document does not have a body, it is still allowed (and it's recommended) to have a `<head>` tag. The `<title>` tag is still used to populate the title bar of the browser window, which will use this single title until the frameset is left. It is still possible to use other head-related tags in the document, such as meta tags and keywords.

The frameset uses the `cols` or `rows` attributes to divide the browser window. `cols` is used to break the window into columns. `rows` is used to break the window into rows. You can use both at the same time to create more complex framesets. Similar to tables, sizes may be defined as either a fixed amount, by specifying a number of pixels, or as a percentage, by specifying a number between `1` and `99`, including a percent sign. Percentages are based on the height or width of the available space, which is either the browser window or the containing frame (in the case of nested frames).

Additionally, you can specify an asterisk for a value rather than specifying a number of pixels or a percentage. This value tells the browser to use any remaining width or height for this row or column. You can use several asterisks for different values to tell the browser to evenly divide the remaining space among several frames.

Frame tags are used to specify additional information about each frame. Frames are included in order from first row to last, left to right. The browser automatically determines which frame tag refers to which available frame, based on order. The two most important attributes of a frame are its name and source (src). The source of a frame is the document that should appear in that frame when the frameset is loaded into a browser window. This document is replaced when either a link is activated in a frame, or another frame's link replaces the document by using targeting. The name of the frame is used when targeting links between frames. In the case of a simple link using the `<a>` tag, the name of the frame is added as an attribute inside the tag. This tells the browser to load the resulting page into the specified frame instead of the frame in which the link resides.

Nested Framesets

Nested framesets are framesets that appear within other framesets. This is usually done to create frames that don't span the entire height or width of the browser. You can create nested frames in two ways. One is to substitute a frame with a frameset, such as the following:

```
<frameset cols="80,*">
    <frame name="nav" src="nav.htm">
    <frameset rows="100,*">
    <frame name="topnav" src="topnav.htm">
        <frame name="content" src="home.htm">
    </frameset>
</frameset>
```

This code would create a navigation on the left of the window with a width of 80 pixels and an additional navigation area at the top of the window with a height of 100 pixels. The frameset containing the topnav and content frames is said to be nested in the larger frameset.

When the window resizes, changes in the size of each frame is determined by how it is defined. The nav frame will stay the same width (80 pixels) but will change in height with the browser window. The topnav frame will stay 100 pixels high but will stretch in window with the browser window. The content frame will stretch in both height and width along with the browser window.

The second way to create nested framesets is to reference an additional frameset as the document for use within a frame. On loading, the frame will be divided based on the specifications contained in the second frameset.

Nested framesets are often used to get around limitations in frame creation, such as when columns and rows of irregular sizes need to be created.

Although nesting framesets is perfectly valid, you should be aware that sometimes it complicates programming and debugging efforts. Extra care needs to be taken to avoid duplicating frame names in any documents that may be in the browser window at the same time, because this can easily confuse the browser and cause unexpected results. You also need to make sure that the frame you are targeting is always onscreen at any point in which you might target it. If the browser doesn't find the frame you reference, it will put the results into a new window.

Creating Frames in Dreamweaver

Dreamweaver tries to simplify the complexities of dealing with frames. It provides graphical tools that create framesets and frames with minimum effort and makes sure that references between them are maintained. You can create frames in Dreamweaver in two ways—through the Modify menu and through the Objects panel.

When a document is open, you can create a frame by using a command or object. The open document becomes one of the frames in the frameset, usually the main content frame.

Using the Modify Menu

The Modify, Frameset submenu provides basic options for splitting a page into frames and creating related files. The four options are the following:

- Split Frame Left
- Split Frame Right
- Split Frame Up
- Split Frame Down

Each option creates a frameset, using the existing document as the source for the frame in the direction indicated. After this menu is used to create a frameset, the four options are disabled.

> **NOTE**
> After you click into one of the frames, the basic options again become enabled, and you are allowed to nest frames inside each other in this fashion.

A fifth option available on this menu is the Edit NoFrames Content selection. This allows editing of NoFrames content, covered later in this chapter.

Using the Objects Panel

The Frames category of the Objects panel provides a more robust method of creating frames. Eight default frameset options can be applied to an existing document simply by making the appropriate selection in the panel. Unlike the Modify, Frameset submenu, the names in the Frames panel imply the direction of the frame(s) to be added to the document. The existing content document is placed into the remaining frame, as implied by the blue shading in the icons.

Frame objects created in this manner can be nested inside each other or inside frames created with the Modify, Frameset method.

Saving Frames and Framesets

Saving framesets in the correct locations with the correct names can be the trickiest part of using frames within Dreamweaver. When you apply frames to an existing document, Dreamweaver creates additional frames for the file in memory. These files may be edited, but they are not yet saved. Dreamweaver will allow you either to save all the files at one time using File, Save All Frames or save each file one-by-one using the File, Save Frame selection.

To change the frame that is being saved with the File, Save Frame selection, move the cursor into the appropriate frame. When files are saved to the hard drive, Dreamweaver will make sure that the links to the source file are updated in the related frameset file.

To save the frameset file itself, either use the File, Save All Frames option or select the Frameset object in the Frames panel and choose File, Save Frameset. You can also select the Frameset by clicking the thin border that surrounds your preview in the Document window.

Open in Frame

The File, Open in Frame option enables you to swap out the currently selected source file for a frame and replace it with a new one that you select. The newly selected file opens immediately inside the frameset file and will permanently become the default document for this frame.

The Frames Panel

The Frames panel (Window, Frames) shows a high-level conceptualization of the state of the framesets and frames in the currently selected document. The Frames panel enables you to quickly identify the various framesets and frames in your document and select these elements so that they can be manipulated or saved.

Identification

In the Frames panel, each frameset is shown with a thick border of several pixels. Inside, columns and rows are broken out into their approximate relative width and height. If any of the frames contains a frameset, it is shown with a thick border and with each frame sized approximately. The name of each frame is shown centered within its rectangle in the panel.

Selection

Any frameset or frame in the current file can be selected by using the Frames panel. To select a frame, click the rectangle showing its name. To select a frameset, click the thick border that represents that frameset in the Frames panel. If several framesets are in a document, each is separately selectable.

> **TIP**
>
> When a frame is selected in the Frames panel, the parent Frameset(s) are available for selection in the Tag Selector. Use this method if it becomes too difficult to select a frameset border.

Resizing

Framesets can be resized in the Document window by clicking a frameset border and dragging it in the appropriate direction. When you let go after a drag, the dimensions of the new frames will be used to change the frameset code appropriately.

If you are trying to match a particular size or need to change the way the frame is sized (to Pixel, Percent, or Relative), you should use the Properties Inspector. Select the frameset using one of the preceding methods and open the Properties Inspector. The Properties Inspector will show a breakdown of the current frameset on the right, similar to the manner used in the Frames panel. This selector can be used to identify a column or row, which then becomes available for editing. After making a selection, you can modify the value and/or units for sizing.

Creating Frames by Dragging

Documents that are framesets show a thin dotted border in the Design view. This line represents the frameset and can be used to select it for editing its code or properties. Around the document edge, it also can be used to precisely create additional columns or rows. To do this, click and drag the dotted line in a file that already has a frameset, and you should see a new column or row appear.

Properties Inspector Frameset

When a frameset is selected, the Properties Inspector allows manipulation of the basic frameset properties. It also shows how many rows and columns are currently in the frameset. The basic properties are the following:

- Borders—A Yes/No/Default selector enables you to set whether borders should be shown for the frameset.
- Border Color—A color selector or text entry box enables you to set the border color for the borders, if you select to have them shown.
- Border Width—Enables the width or height (depending on the direction) of the border between frames.

Frame sizing can also be manipulated using the Properties Inspector, which is detailed earlier in this chapter in the section "Resizing."

Properties Inspector Frame

When a frame is selected, the Properties Inspector allows manipulation of properties related to the frame. Because frame sizes are stored as part of the frameset, not as part of the frame, you must manipulate the frameset to change the widths or heights of related frames.

The following properties can be manipulated in the Properties Inspector when a frame is selected:

- Frame Name—The frame name is important because it is used with the target attribute in `<a>` and `<form>` tags.
- Source (Src)—This is the name of the source file that populates the frame. It can be typed, selected, or redirected here. You can use the Open File button to use a dialog box, or use the pointer icon to select a file from the Site window.
- Scroll—Scrolling for each frame can be controlled with this setting. Options are Yes, No, Auto, or Default. Auto scrolling enables a scrollbar to appear if it is needed to display the contents at the frame size; otherwise, it hides it. This is the default of most modern browsers.
- No Resize—Prevents the user from resizing the frame column or row in the browser.

- Borders—Allows the borders to be turned on for a particular frame.
- Border Color—This color selector and text entry field allows a border color to be chosen.

NoFrames

When developing a great-looking site, it is easy to forget that not everyone is browsing the Web using the same technology that you are using. With frames, three common problems occur:

- Users are using older browsers that can't view frames.
- Users are using new technology that can't view frames to browse the Web.
- Users are using various devices to handicap-enable the Web, some of which can't navigate frames.

To avoid alienating your target users, consider adding NoFrames content to your site. NoFrames content is a normal HTML page that is added inside the frameset document, below the frameset tag. On a simple site, the NoFrames content may be an alternative copy of the information, formatted without frames. At the very least, you should provide users with an alternative way to get to the information, such as phone, mail, or e-mail.

To edit the NoFrames content, choose Modify, Frameset, Edit NoFrames Content. You will be switched to a Design mode in which you can add a short or long message to the document for your users. To return to the frameset, choose Modify, Frameset, Edit NoFrames Content again.

After adding your NoFrames content, your frameset might look like the following:

```
<html>
<head>
    <title>My Site</title>
</head>

<frameset cols="80,*">
    <frame name="nav" src="navigation.htm">
    <frame name="content" src="home.htm">
</frameset>
<noframes>
<body bgcolor="#FFFFFF">
<p>Sorry, you need a frames-capable browser to view our site.</p>
<p>Please call 1-888-555-0199 for a free catalog.</p>
</body>
</noframes>
</html>
```

Summary

Framesets are used to break up the browser window into columns and rows, making frames. Each frame in a frameset refers to an individual document, which is displayed in the specified portion of the screen. Frame names are used to refer to a specific frame when linking to new pages.

Framesets are a controversial part of Web development, having many advantages and disadvantages. If you decide to use frames in your site, you should make sure that you provide a useful source of alternative information using the `<noframes>` tag.

Templates and Library Links are tools that can be used to reuse information across your site and to synchronize the navigation to your site. These technologies are specifically a part of the Dreamweaver tool.

Sample Questions

1. What tag allows alternate information to be shown to people who cannot read frames in their browser?
   A. `<frameless>`
   B. `<noframesets>`
   C. `<noframes>`
   D. `<alt>`

2. Framesets can reference other framesets as frames.
   A. True
   B. False

3. Which is an advantage of frames?
   A. Manages user security
   B. Content can reside on different servers seamlessly
   C. Easier for all Web browsers to read
   D. Keeps a common style sheet for all content

CHAPTER 14

Formatting with Cascading Style Sheets

Introduction

Cascading style sheets (CSS) represent a revolution still in the making in Web development. Many sites now use CSS, although few use style sheets as extensively as they probably should.

A good portion of CSS1, the first CSS specification approved by the W3C, is supported by all browsers in use, in versions 4.0 and later (Internet Explorer and Opera support some of CSS1 in 3.x versions). CSS positioning, part of CSS2, is also supported in 4.0 and later browsers.

What CSS provides is a way of separating display rule specifications from document structure. There are two significant advantages in doing this:

- Specifying and maintaining the look and feel of the site is much easier; because you can create one set of style rules for an entire site, you do not have to worry about the consistency of formatting across the site. In addition, changing the look and feel of the site requires only the editing of a single style sheet.
- Site content can easily be repurposed for delivery in other contexts and media; you can use different style sheets for different browsers (controlling which one is used through browser detection and writing the link to the style sheet dynamically via server- or client-side scripting). You can also use different style sheets for creating PDF or Word versions of the pages or for deploying them in nonbrowser Internet devices such as PDAs and wireless phones.

The future of HTML, if developers follow the specifications, will entail more proliferation and exhaustive use of CSS. The strict form of HTML 4.01 and XHTML require a complete separation of document structure from display specification, the latter delegated to style sheets. This means that tags such as `<font>` and `<center>` and attributes such as `align`, `bgcolor`, and `cellpadding` are not allowed. No browser enforces this separation at present, of course, but developers can benefit from adhering to it.

Macromedia Dreamweaver provides an excellent CSS editor that requires no familiarity with CSS syntax and properties and exposes only those properties that have general browser support.

In this chapter, we look at the central concepts of CSS and its implementation in Dreamweaver.

CSS Syntax

The basic syntax for all CSS style rules is the same:

```
Selector {property1:value;property2:value...}
```

Following is an example that defines a rule for `<h1>` headings:

```
h1 {font-size: 22px; font-family: arial,sans-serif; color: #330033}
```

> **TIP**
>
> If you edit style sheets outside of Dreamweaver, be aware that the most common coding error is omitting the semicolon (;) separator between property/value pairs. If a style sheet is not functioning properly, this is the first thing to look for; it is often difficult to find because the error may not occur in the rule you notice that is not being applied. A missing semicolon will invalidate all subsequent rules in the style sheet because the CSS interpreter will read all remaining code as a continuation of the unterminated property value.

The rule itself—the property/value pairs between the braces—will take the same form in all cases. Table 14.1 shows several kinds of selectors:

Table 14.1 CSS Selector Types

Selector	Example	Description
[Tag]	p	Any HTML or XML tag name, without the surrounding <> brackets. For XHTML, the tag name must be in lowercase.
Group	`p, td, li`	Multiple tag names in a comma-delimited list that all use the same style rule.

Table 14.1 continued

Selector	Example	Description
Contextual	`td, p, em`	The style rule is applied to a tag only when it occurs in a particular context. In the example, the rule will be applied to an `em` tag only if it is nested inside a paragraph that is nested inside a table data cell.
Custom class	`.highlight`	The rule is applied only to elements having the attribute `class="[classname]"` (example: `class="highlight"`). If a tag name precedes the classname (example: `p.highlight`), the class can be applied only to that tag.
ID	`#layer1`	The rule is applied only to the element having the attribute `id="[IDname]"` (example: `id="layer1"`). An id value may be used only once in a particular page.
Pseudo-class	`a:link`	The rule applies to an element in a particular state. In the example, the rule would be applied to <a> tags used for hyperlinks that the user has not visited.
Pseudo-element	`p:first-line`	The rule is applied only to a portion of the element, such as the first line or first letter of a block.

The most commonly used selector types will be discussed in more detail in later sections of this chapter.

> **CAUTION**
>
> A tag selector should be used only once in a style sheet and should not appear in a group selector if it exists as an ordinary tag selector.
>
> Also remember that IDs are intended to identify a unique element in the page, so no two tags in the same page should have the same id value—if they do, JavaScript code that refers to the elements will not function properly. To apply a special custom style to multiple elements on the same page, use classes instead. ID style rules are ideal for layers used in page layout, however.

In Dreamweaver's CSS editor, you can create tag rules in the New Style dialog box (Text, CSS Styles, New Style) by selecting Redefine HTML tag. You can create custom classes by selecting Make Custom Style. ID, Pseudo-Class, Pseudo-Element, and Contextual rules are created by choosing CSS selectors and then choosing a Pseudo-Class selector from the drop-down list or typing one of the other selector types into the selector field.

You cannot create Group selector rules directly in Dreamweaver, but you can do so by editing the style sheet in a text editor such as HomeSite or a CSS editor such as TopStyle.

Custom Classes

Custom classes help to make your style sheets and HTML much more flexible. CSS classes allow you to use a single HTML tag for a variety of purposes by defining different display rules appropriate to each use. The following code sample shows how CSS classes could be applied to cells in a table of products, applying different styles to the name, description, and price information:

CSS code:

```
.productname {
     background-color : #F0E68C;
     font-weight : bold;
     font-size : 14px;
     color : #8B4513;
}
.productdescription {
     font-style : italic;
     font-size : 10px;
}
.productprice {
     font-size : 12px;
     background-color : #EEE8AA;
}
```

HTML code:

```
<table cellspacing="0" cellpadding="5">
    <tr>
      <td class="productname">Mocha Java</td>
      <td class="productdescription">A smooth, classic blend, perfect for an
        afternoon cup </td>
      <td class="productprice">$10.95/LB</td>
    </tr>
    <tr>
      <td class="productname">French Roast</td>
      <td class="productdescription">A deep, rich dark roast, good for a
       morning jumpstart or made espresso-style with dessert</td>
      <td class="productprice">$11.95/LB</td>
    </tr>
  </table>
```

> **TIP**
>
> When you use classes in this way, name them as you would name XML tags if you were building an XML language for your content. This will make both the CSS and HTML code easier to understand. An additional benefit is that if you actually write the XML tag set, all you will have to do is remove the periods from the class names, and your style sheet will work for the XML code.

All class names in the style sheet must begin with a period (.), which is not included when the class is referenced using the class attribute in your HTML code. You can include as many classes as you like and reuse them as many times as you like in a page or across a site.

If the class name is preceded by a tag name (for example, `p.productname`), the class is specific to that tag. Otherwise, any class may be applied to any tag.

When you define a tag rule for a tag and also apply a class to the tag, the properties are cumulative, but where the same property is used in both rules, the class property value takes precedence:

```
td {
     font-size : 11px;
     color : #333399;
}
.productdescription {
     font-style : italic;
     font-size : 10px;
}
...
<td class="productdescription">
Fruity, with light oak overtones and a citrus finish
</td>
```

In the preceding example, the complete style rule for the table data element would be the following:

```
{
     color : #333399;
     font-style : italic;
     font-size : 10px;
}
```

> **TIP**
>
> To make your style sheets easy to extend and maintain over the life of the site, it is important to give some thought to how you assign style properties, especially for tag and class rules. The tag rule should represent the least common denominator for the display style of all content that will be contained in that tag. Classes should add style properties that are specific to various kinds of content.

> If you define a lengthy list of properties in the tag rule for what is actually an eccentric kind of content, you will then have to add extra properties to your classes to override property values in the tag rule that are not appropriate for most content.

CSS Selectors

The CSS selector option in the Dreamweaver New Style dialog box allows you to create rules with selectors other than simple tag or class selectors. The drop-down list for the field includes only the pseudo-classes for the <a> tag, but you can type pseudo-element (for example, `p:first-line`), ID (for example, `#maincontent`), and contextual (for example, h1 strong) selectors into the field.

The first-letter and first-line pseudo-elements are well supported in Internet Explorer 5.0 and later and Netscape 6 and later, although the rendering is slightly different. You may need to use a negative bottom margin in Netscape to get the first-letter character positioned correctly.

ID selectors must begin with a pound (#) sign, which is not included when the ID value is referenced in an HTML id attribute. IDs are generally used as unique identifiers for HTML elements in DHTML to allow a script to manipulate properties of a particular element in response to some event. IDs must be unique within the page.

Linking Style Sheets

In general, the most efficient way to use style sheets is in a separate CSS file. This file will have the extension .css and will contain no HTML code.

A separate style sheet is attached to a page using the `<link>` tag, which should be placed inside the `<head>` tag:

```
<head>
<title>ANDES</title>
<link rel="stylesheet" href="/test.css" type="text/css">
</head>
```

More than one style sheet can be attached to a single page. In keeping with the general rule of top-down processing of HTML code, multiple linked style sheets are processed in order, and each one takes precedence over style sheets that were processed earlier, if a property for the same rule is defined more than once.

Embedding Style Sheets

In addition to or instead of linking a style sheet using the `<link>` tag, you can embed a style sheet in a page. For embedded style sheets, all CSS code must be nested inside an HTML `<style>` tag:

```
<style>
a {
```

```
    color : #B22222;
    text-decoration : none;
}

a:hover {
    color : #1E90FF;
    text-decoration : underline;
}
td {
    font-size : 11px;
    color : #333399;
}
</style>
```

> **TIP**
>
> There are, in general, only two good reasons to use an embedded style sheet instead of a linked one: if the page has highly eccentric display specifications not found anywhere else on the site or if you are working inside someone else's template and cannot apply an external style sheet.
>
> If neither of these conditions applies, you should probably use an external style sheet rather than an embedded one.

Inline Styles

Inline styles are applied to specific tags by embedding CSS code in the value of an HTML tag style attribute:

```
<p style="color:#999999;font-size:12pt">
```

Generally, this is the least desirable way of applying CSS styles, because nothing is gained over using the formatting attributes of HTML except the broader set of style properties in CSS.

> **CAUTION**
>
> The style attribute has been deprecated in the XHTML specification. It is likely to be removed from the specification eventually.

> **TIP**
>
> You should use inline styles only when the CSS code is unique to a single element or when you cannot link or embed a style sheet because you are working within a template over which you have no control.

Cascading Order

In some cases, you may specify different style features for the same text through a combination of a linked style sheet, an embedded style tag, and inline style attributes.

If these different specifications conflict with one another, the browser must decide which value to use. The choice is made on the basis of an order of precedence (this is the cascading order that gives CSS its name).

The order of precedence for CSS is as follows:

- Inline style attributes take precedence over embedded style tags.
- Embedded style tags, in turn, take precedence over linked style sheets.

It is important to remember this order of precedence so that you'll know which style values will override others. Rather than worrying about the rule, however, it may be easier just to remember that the style definition closest to the HTML element takes precedence over rules that are farther away.

When style properties defined in linked, embedded, and inline style rules do not conflict, they are cumulative.

Inheritance

Inheritance is similar to cascading order but applies to HTML tags that are nested inside other tags:

```
<h1><strong>Very</strong> important heading</h1>
```

The nested element inherits the style properties of the parent element in addition to its own. If the style properties conflict, those of the nested element take precedence over those of the parent.

An additional complication is that some properties cannot be inherited. This is part of the design of CSS because inheritance of some properties would be a problem rather than a help.

To see whether a property is inherited, you can consult the complete CSS Reference that is included in Dreamweaver.

Summary

- Cascading style sheets (CSS) provide a way of separating the display characteristics of a document from its logical structure, which is defined using HTML.
- The HTML specifications are moving in the direction of strictly mandating the separation of display specifications from the document structure; the strict DTDs (document type definitions, which define the syntax rules for a markup language) for HTML 4.01 and XHTML already do so.
- All CSS rules have the same syntax: a selector combined with a set of property/value pairs.
- There are several types of selectors; the most commonly used are tag, class, and id selectors.
- CSS styles can be applied through linked style sheets, embedded style sheets and inline styles.

- If styles for the same element are defined in more than one place, the properties are cumulative, but those closest to the element take precedence.
- Nested elements inherit some, but not all, style properties from their parent elements.

Sample Questions

1. Which of the following is a valid id selector?
   A. `.layer1`
   B. `#layer1`
   C. `id_layer1`
   D. `h1_layer1`

2. Which line of the following CSS code contains an error?

```
1    td em {
2            font-size: 12pt;
3            color: red
4            background-color: silver;
5            font-family: sans-serif
6         }
```

   A. Line 1
   B. Line 2
   C. Line 3
   D. There are no errors in the code.

Sample Questions

PART III

REUSE, COLLABORATION, AND AUTOMATION

CHAPTER 15

Site Assets

Resources used on Web pages often come from different sources. Web designers design images and define color palettes; designers and developers create Macromedia Flash movies; and Web developers develop JavaScript scripts. This work is often done prior to the actual development of the site. You can begin development by collecting all these assets into one convenient place for use while you develop—the Assets panel.

Assets Panel

Site assets are arranged and managed using the Assets panel. The panel displays the assets in your site, dividing them into several categories, such as images, colors, URLs, and Flash movies.

You can display the Assets panel using the Window, Assets menu item.

You will see two views of your assets in the panel: the Site list, and your Favorites list.

The Site list is built from all files defined in your site that match one of the asset categories. This happens automatically. It also includes all colors and URLs that are used in any document in your site.

> **NOTE**
>
> You must define a site and create a site cache before you can use the Assets panel.

You build the Favorites list when you explicitly move commonly used assets into the list.

In both lists, assets are divided into categories; you choose which category of assets to list by clicking one of the category buttons.

Asset Categories

Table 15.1 shows the categories of assets available.

Table 15.1 Asset Categories

Category	Description
Images	Image files in GIF, JPEG, or PNG format.
Colors	Colors used in any documents or style sheets in your site, including text, background, and link colors.
URLs	External URLs defined within your site pages. Includes all types of links.
Flash movies	Files in Macromedia Flash's format (SWF files).
Shockwave movies	Files in Macromedia Shockwave's format.
MPEG and QuickTime movies	Movies in QuickTime or MPEG format.
Scripts	JavaScript or VBScript files.
Templates	Reusable page layout files.
Library items	Reusable elements referenced on many pages.

NOTE

All categories are available on both lists, except templates and library items.

Click the appropriate category icon and click either Site or Favorites. For example, to display all the colors in your site, click the Colors icon and then click Site.

There are several times when assets will not appear immediately. To force the new assets to appear, refresh the Site list.

Adding an Asset to a Page

You can preview an asset in the Assets panel before using it. Click the asset, and a visual preview of the asset is displayed. When a movie asset is selected, the preview area shows an icon. You can use the Play button to preview the movie.

You can insert most kinds of assets into your document by dragging them into the Document window. You can also use the Insert button. Templates are applied to the entire document and therefore cannot be dragged in. Templates are discussed in Chapter 17, "Using Templates."

Maintaining Assets

You can use mouse clicks (with Shift and Ctrl keys on Windows and the Command key on Macintosh) to select many assets at a time. This also enables you to edit many assets at a time. Double-click the asset and then click Edit.

Some kinds of assets invoke an external editing application. For colors and URLs, you can change the asset only in the Favorites list. You can use Edit, Preferences to add external editors for file types.

Favorites

A favorite is a resource or element that you commonly use throughout your site or in sections of your site. The Site list can become cumbersome in its long list of resources, many of which you many never want to reuse. By creating a favorite out of an asset, you can easily find reusable components.

Adding and Removing Favorites

Click Favorites at the top of the Assets panel to display any favorites you have chosen. This list is empty until you add assets to it. To make an asset a favorite, select it in the Site list and then click the Add to Favorites button.

> **NOTE**
> Favorites are stored as references to the Site list, not as separate files. Macromedia Dreamweaver keeps track of which assets from the Site list to display in the Favorites list.

To remove a Favorite, simply select one or more assets and click the Remove from Favorites button while you are in the Favorites view.

There are several tasks that you can perform only in the Favorites list. These tasks include the following:

- Grouping of favorites
- Applying nicknames to favorites

Favorites Nicknames

You can give nicknames to assets in the Favorites list. The nickname is displayed instead of the asset's filename or value. For example, if you have a color named `#999900`, you might use a more descriptive nickname, such as `MainWindowBGColor` or `HighlightTextColor`. Only Favorites can be assigned nicknames; the Site list uses the real values.

To give a nickname to a favorite asset, select the asset's name or icon in the Assets panel, right-click (Windows) or Control+click (Macintosh) and choose Edit Nickname.

Grouping Assets in a Favorites Folder

In the Favorites list, within a given category, you can create named groups of assets, called Favorites folders. For instance, you may want to group all images for a university faculty under a folder called Faculty.

> **NOTE**
>
> Placing an asset in a Favorites folder does not change the location of the asset's file on your disk.

Use the New Favorites Folder button on the Favorites list panel and give it a name. Then drag assets into that folder for grouping.

Working with Assets and Sites

You can locate the original asset in the Site Manager, as long as it is a file asset (not a color or a URL). Right-click (Windows) or Control+click (Macintosh) on the asset item and select Locate in Site.

> **NOTE**
>
> The Assets panel is associated with the active document. Therefore, the Site window may not correspond to the Assets panel. Check the panel's title bar to determine the site.

You can use this feature to help copy an asset to another site or to the remote site. You can copy an individual asset, a set of assets, or an entire Favorites folder at once.

Select what you would like to copy and choose Copy to Site from the context menu. After you choose the target site, Dreamweaver creates a mirror of the directory structure for the newly copied asset in the target site if it doesn't already exist. Colors and URLs are added only to the Favorites list.

Summary

Dreamweaver enables you to display all site assets in an organized manner in the Assets panel. It automatically categorizes nine types of assets and scans the defined site for assets in those categories. In this way, you can quickly reuse colors, URLs, images, and movie files on many pages in your site. It also allows you to get even more control by creating a list of favorites and allows intuitive grouping and nicknaming of those assets.

Sample Questions

1. Which of the following elements on the Assets panel cannot be dragged into a page?
   A. Images
   B. Colors
   C. Templates
   D. Images

2. The Assets panel displays assets from all defined sites.
   A. True
   B. False

CHAPTER 16

Library Items and Extensions

What Are Library Items?

When designing and building a Web site, you will frequently need to copy the same section of code over and over. Frequently this happens because an item is used in navigation that might appear on multiple pages, such as a menu or submenu. As a developer, if you use simple copy-and-paste methods to move the code, you are opening the door to integrity problems down the line. You'll need, for instance, to remember to update each copy of the code when changes are made. You'll also need a way to communicate to others on your team about where changes should be made when common code is updated.

In HTML and in Macromedia Dreamweaver, there are many ways to solve this problem when it arises. For now, we are going to talk about the most powerful and flexible method for doing this—the use of Library Items.

Library Items are sections of code, saved into a discrete file and managed with the help of Dreamweaver. Library Items are managed by Dreamweaver so that all copies of the code look the same. When the Library Item needs to be updated, Dreamweaver searches for all uses of the code and updates them.

Library Items are browsed and manipulated as part of the Site Assets panel. You can view the Library Items in your current site by selecting Library from the Window menu.

Advantages of Library Items

Library Items have many advantages to them, including the following:

- The capability to easily manage identical pieces of code, no matter where they fall in your site.
- The capability to share Library Items with other developers on your team.
- The capability to detach the Library Item from its original to create a variation of the item.
- Library Items do not require any special server software to run.
- Files that use Library Items contain all HTML so that any other editor can read and manipulate them.
- Library Items can be moved from site to site to automate the development process.
- Library Items are easy to manage and maintain, even with a large number of developers, because of Dreamweaver's built-in tools.

Drawbacks of Library Items

Although other HTML editing tools can read and manipulate files with Library Items, you do not get Dreamweaver's synchronization features in these other tools.

Library Items work best on blocks of code that will be identical each time they are used. Blocks of code that need to be customized with each use don't work as well as Library Items.

Related Techniques

Some other techniques exist for reusing content that give similar results. You should be aware of all your options when deciding to use a technology to automate development. These techniques are

- Server-Side Includes—These refer to external files that are added to an HTML file by the Web server at the time the file is requested by a browser. They are more dependent on the Web server than Library Items are, and they are not available in all cases.
- Templates—These are another Dreamweaver-specific tool for automating the development of Web sites. Templates are best used when a majority of the page is going to stay the same. They are not as flexible with the placement of reusable objects as Library Items are.
- New Objects—You can create new objects in the Objects panel by saving HTML to your hard drive. These objects can contain simple HTML that you can then use across all your sites.
- Application Includes—Some application servers include options for dynamically inserting smaller HTML files into a larger document. One popular tool is ColdFusion, which uses the `<CFInclude>` tag. This tag allows includes from anywhere in the domain and allows included files to contain additional ColdFusion code.

> **NOTE**
>
> Server-side includes rely on the Web server to find and include them when a page is requested. They are not a more popular technique, because Web servers handle them differently and have different requirements regarding their use. For instance, some Web servers limit their use to files ending in SHTML, whereas others won't allow files in parent directories to be included.

Creating a Library Item

You create Library Items by selecting target code that you want to turn into a Library Item and choosing Modify, Library, Add Object to Library. This takes the code selected in the Design window and copies it into an unnamed Library Item. You can name the Library Item at that time. It also identifies the code in the Design window as referencing a Library Item, which then makes it directly uneditable.

You can also create blank Library Items by opening the Library category of the Site Assets panel and selecting New Library Item from the pull-down arrow. This creates a new blank Library Item that you can name, open, and add content to.

Editing a Library Item

Library Items in your site may not be directly edited in the Design window. To edit them, you need to open the original Library Item and do your editing there. Then you'll be able to update the pages of your site to include the changes.

> **NOTE**
>
> You could edit the Library Item in the Design window if you open up the Code view. In it, you'll be able to modify the Library Item's HTML code directly. This isn't recommended, however, because any changes you make by directly manipulating the code will be wiped out if the Library Item changes in the future.

When you have the Library Item selected in the Design view, you will be able to open the original by clicking the Open button on the Properties Inspector. You can also right-click the Library Item and select Open Library Item to achieve the same result.

> **TIP**
>
> Library Items can be placed anywhere, including inside templates and even in other Library Items.

To open a Library Item that is not in your current document, you can either open the related file from the Library folder in your Site File window, or use the Site Assets panel to select and open the file. These two techniques are covered in more detail later in the chapter.

When you open a Library Item, it appears in a separate window. The title of the window will include the words <<<Library Item>>> to remind you that you are not editing a normal HTML page. The filename of the Library Item will always end in lbi. Because Library Items are independent blocks of HTML, they do not contain all the tags that would allow them to appear as a unified part of your site. For instance, Library Items have no <body> tags, so they appear on a gray background, and they don't have cascading style sheet calls, so they appear using default styles and colors.

After you have the Library Item document open, you can edit it using any of the regular Dreamweaver objects and tools. Remember that the item will look slightly different in this mode than it will look on your finished page.

To update a changed Library Item across your site, simply close the window after making your changes. You will be asked to save the changes to the file containing the Library Item. If you choose to do so, Dreamweaver will search your site and ask if it should update files that it finds that use your item. If you choose to update these files, your changes will be propagated throughout your entire site.

Detaching a Library Item

If you need to modify individual uses of a Library Item, you may need to detach it from the original. Detaching a Library Item releases it from being updated when the original is updated and also allows the item to become directly modifiable in the Design view. Essentially, this process returns it to being normal HTML code again.

To detach a Library Item, select it in the Design view and, using the Properties Inspector, click the Detach from Original button. You can also right-click the Library Item and select Detach from Original from the pop-up menu.

Updating a Library Item

Sometimes when using Library Items, you will find that a use of the Library Item no longer matches the original item. This can happen because you chose not to update all items when making changes, because another team member has made changes to an item while you were editing files, or because you made some changes directly to the HTML that you need to revert.

In any case, you can update a Library Item within your page by clicking it and in the Properties Inspector clicking the Recreate button. This will copy the Original Library Item code back over the code representing your copy in the current document. You can also right-click the Library Item and select Recreate from the pop-up menu.

Updating All Items in a Document

If you know or suspect that several items in your page are out of sync with their Library Items, you can update all the items in that document. To do this, you choose Modify, Library, Update Current Page while in the Design view of the Document window. This causes Dreamweaver to synchronize each item in your file with the original Library Item.

Updating All Items in a Site

To update all items across your site at once, use the Update Pages option. To select this option, choose Modify, Library, Update Pages while a document from your site is open. This brings up the Update Pages dialog box, which is used to customize how the updates should be performed and to give you a log of the updates completed.

You can choose to update Library Items, Templates, or both. You can also select updates for specific Library Items or Templates. Choosing Start begins the process and generates a log in the lower pane.

About the Storage of Library Items

Library Items are always stored in a folder titled Library off the root of the site directory. Each Library Item filename is generated from the name given the item when it was created. These files are viewable and modifiable in the Site Files window. Changes made to the filenames using the Site Files window will alter the names used to refer to the Library Item in your site. Recognizing the potential for problems, Dreamweaver will prompt you to update your site to reflect these changes. You should choose to make these changes unless you have a reason not to. Not updating your site will cause broken links to occur in your site. You should also be aware that changes made to Library Item filenames are not always reflected immediately in the Site Assets panel, sometimes creating a need to re-create the site list.

Library Items can be transferred up to a site—and should be the potential exists for others to need those files. This is covered in more detail in Chapter 22, "Transferring Files to Remote Servers."

Managing Library Items with the Site Assets Panel

The best way to change filenames and manage Library Items is to use the Site Assets panel. This enables you to change names and update your site, all while keeping the site assets list in order.

Open the Library category in the Site Assets panel by choosing Window, Library from the menu. You will see a preview area, a list of selectable Library Items, and some tools to help manage items.

Creating Library Items

New Library Items can be created by selecting the New Library Item button at the bottom of the panel or by selecting the New Library Item option from the arrow pull-down menu.

After creating a new item, you can name it. That name is then used as a basis for the filename. All Library Items are placed in the Site's Library folder, off the site root.

To begin adding content to your new Library Item, you can either double-click the item itself or, while it is selected, click the Edit button at the bottom of the panel. You can also double-click in the preview area. Any of these options will open the Library Item file and allow you to begin adding content.

Renaming Library Items

When you rename Library Items, you are renaming the filename used to hold the item as well as the links in each of your site files used to refer to the Library Item. You can rename a Library Item by selecting the Rename option from the arrow pull-down menu while the item is selected. When you rename an item, Dreamweaver automatically renames the file associated with the item and allows you to update references to this item across your site.

> **TIP**
>
> Dreamweaver will let you name your Library Item using almost any typeable characters. Because the name is also used as the filename, you can potentially cause problems for yourself when moving the files. To play it safe, you should use only letters, numbers, and the underscore when naming your library items.

Deleting Library Items

You can delete Library Items by selecting them and pressing the Delete button at the bottom of the panel. You can also delete items by selecting the item and choosing Delete from the arrow pull-down menu.

Deleting Library Items erases the file from the Library folder in the root of your site. It does not delete references to the Library Item in your site for you, however. This means that any pages using the Library Item will still expect a Library Item to exist when you edit them. Unless you are intentionally swapping one Library Item for another, you should avoid deleting Library Items that are being used in your site. If you run across a reference to a deleted Library Item in your site, you can use the Detach from Original button on the Properties Inspector to unhook the reference and return it to normal HTML.

Refreshing the List

When the list of current Library Items becomes out of date, you will need to refresh the list. This can happen because files were changed or moved outside of Dreamweaver or because item names were changed directly in the Site window.

To refresh the Site list, select Refresh Site List from the bottom of the panel or choose Refresh Site List from the arrow pull-down menu. This process will update the Assets panel to use the most current information.

Adding Items to Your Documents

You can use your Library Items in any HTML file, including templates. To add a Library Item to an open document, simply drag the item off the Site Assets panel and place it into your document. You can also position the cursor in your document, select the desired Library Item in the Site Assets panel, and click the Insert button from the bottom of the panel.

Modifying the Objects Panel

The Objects panel and its categories in Dreamweaver is fully customizable to suit the evolving needs of a Web developer. Categories can be added, moved, and renamed, depending on your needs. Objects can be deleted, moved, or even created within these categories. The basis for this is that the Objects panel is really a collection of folders and files sitting inside the Dreamweaver installation directory. By manipulating the organization of the Objects folder (which is contained in the Configuration folder in the Dreamweaver installation directory), you can directly manipulate the interface of the Objects panel.

Adding Objects

Objects added to the Control panel should be saved as .htm files within the desired folder (each folder name equates to a category within the panel). When Dreamweaver is restarted, or when the extensions are forced to reload, the objects appear as icons in the proper category. If a GIF file of the same name is placed in the same directory, Dreamweaver will use that image file to represent the object in the panel.

In a few ways, this technique is different from creating Library Items. For instance, objects added to the Objects panel can be used across all sites at the given workstation. The objects also can contain JavaScript interfaces that allow the user to assign properties to the object as it is inserted. After an object is inserted, however, it is independently modifiable by the user. Unlike Library Items, objects are not synchronized when changes are made to the original copy. And object files, unlike Library Items, are also not automatically uploaded to the production server for sharing among team members.

Extensions

Dreamweaver functionality can be extended with a combination of HTML and JavaScript coding. When a unique feature and its files are packaged for distribution onto other machines, an extension is born. Extensions can be installed onto machines, disabled, and deleted as needed by the developer. Extensions are managed by a common tool called the Macromedia Extension Manager. This tool, which is a separate application from Dreamweaver, allows extensions to be plugged in. The same tool is also used for plugging in extensions to Macromedia Flash.

To load an extension, also known as an MXP file, you can download it to your hard drive and double-click it. This should bring up the file in the Macromedia Extension Manager. You can also load the extension directly into Dreamweaver by double-clicking it.

Installed extensions add functionality in different ways. Usually they will extend the Commands menu or the Insert menu. Some will add objects to the Objects panel.

Others will change Dreamweaver in less obvious ways. See the documentation specific to each extension you install.

Because Dreamweaver loads all the available extensions when it is launched, you will not immediately be able to see the effects of any new extensions. To see the new extensions, you need to exit Dreamweaver and relaunch it. Optionally, you can force Dreamweaver to reload all extensions by Ctrl+clicking (Option-clicking on the Macintosh) the category selector on the Objects panel and choosing Reload Extensions. This will reload fresh copies of all existing extensions into memory and allow you to immediately use their functionality.

> **TIP**
>
> The best place to find new extensions is at macromedia.com. Select Commands, Get More Commands in Dreamweaver, or you can go directly to the following URL:
>
> `http://www.macromedia.com/exchange/dreamweaver/`

Summary

Dreamweaver Library Items provide a great way to reuse content throughout your site and to automate production for other developers, who can use these items as well. Library Items are managed through the Library Category of the Site Assets panel and are kept in the site root in a folder labeled Library.

Functionality can be added to Dreamweaver by the use of extensions, which can be installed on a workstation using the Macromedia Extension Manager. Extensions can be added, disabled, and removed from workstations. Extensions can be used on any site accessible from that workstation, but they do not become a part of the site in the same way a Library Item does.

Sample Questions

1. What is the name of the folder containing Library Items in a site?
   A. Libs
   B. Library
   C. Library_Items
   D. Items

2. The extension MXP refers to what type of file?
   A. Library Item
   B. HTML with JavaScript
   C. Macromedia Extension
   D. Object Panel Object

3. When you modify a Library Item file, Dreamweaver will want to:
   A. Save it as a new filename
   B. Synchronize uses of the Library Item in the site
   C. Create a new template to hold the Library Item
   D. Move the file back to your remote server

CHAPTER 17

Using Templates

Introduction

The Macromedia Dreamweaver Templates feature is a powerful tool for simplifying site maintenance and for distributing authorship of site content among less[nd]technically-savvy colleagues.

Most Web document editors include template capability to allow you to embed code and content that is common to multiple pages. Dreamweaver templates have two important differences from most templates, however:

- Changes made to a template can be cascaded automatically through some or all pages created from the template.
- Areas within the template can be designated as editable or noneditable so that content providers can add content to pages without modifying code that should be constant across pages.

This chapter reviews the creation, use, and updating of templates, as well as the use of tracing images as visual guides for creating new templates.

Using Tracing Images

The task of designing the look and feel of a site is often delegated to a graphic artist who creates a visual mock-up of the page and passes it off to an HTML developer. The HTML developer then reproduces the effect of the page image in HTML code.

Dreamweaver makes this common task much easier by allowing you to attach a tracing image to a page. The tracing image is visible when you are editing the page in Dreamweaver, but it is not visible when the page is viewed in a browser.

Any image can be used as a tracing image, as long as it is in one of the standard Web image formats: GIF, JPG, or PNG. Images in other formats can easily be converted to one of these formats using Macromedia Fireworks or another graphics editor.

> **TIP**
>
> If you use Macromedia Fireworks, create and save tracing images in PNG format; this will retain editing features, such as layers, that are lost when you export the image as a GIF or a JPG file.

Tracing images are attached to documents through the Page Properties dialog box, which is accessed through the Modify menu. You can change or remove a tracing image at any time. Because the tracing image is attached through a link, changes to the source image will be automatically reflected in the tracing image. (If the page is currently open in Dreamweaver, you may need to refresh it to see changes in the tracing image.)

In addition to specifying the tracing image, you can also set margins in the Page Properties so that the image will be flush with the top and left edges of the page. You can also adjust the transparency of the image.

> **TIP**
>
> By default, the transparency of the tracing image is set to 100%. This may be confusing to developers because it appears that the elements of the tracing image are actually part of the page. To avoid confusion, try setting the transparency to 50%.

After a tracing image is attached to a page, you can easily create the page layout by drawing layout table cells or layers over appropriate parts of the image. Creating page layouts is covered in Chapter 6, "Using Layers for Page Layout," and Chapter 7, "Using Tables for Page Layout."

Creating Templates

After you have created a page layout in an ordinary HTML page, you can create a Dreamweaver template from the page by selecting File, Save as Template. You provide a name for the template, and Dreamweaver automatically saves the template in a templates folder under the site root. The template will have the filename you specified and the special extension .dwt (for Dreamweaver template).

> **NOTE**
>
> To take advantage of Dreamweaver templates, you must create a site and work within it.
>
> You can create as many templates as you like for a site.

By default, no area of the page created from a template can be edited. Before using the template, you need to define its editable regions.

Creating Editable Regions

After you have created a template and have it open in Dreamweaver, you can select any portion of the page and use the Modify, Templates menu to create an editable region corresponding to the selection. You are prompted to supply a name for each editable region, and the name is required.

The editable region will be highlighted with its name displayed both in the template and in pages created using the template. You can change the colors for highlighting using the Highlighting section of the Preferences (under the Edit menu).

> **CAUTION**
>
> If the selected area that you turn into an editable region has no content, Dreamweaver inserts the name of the region as content. You may want to remove this text from the template because content providers using the template may forget to. Because the editable region has a highlighted border, the text is not needed to identify it visually.

Dreamweaver identifies editable regions through special HTML comments that will not be visible in the page unless a user views the source. The following is an example of code for an editable region:

```
<!-- #BeginEditable "bodycontent" -->
  <div id="layer1">
    <h1 align="left"> </h1>

  </div>
<!-- #EndEditable -->
```

Creating New Pages from Templates

After editable regions have been defined, a template is ready for use. Developers create new pages from a template by selecting File, New from Template. Dreamweaver displays a list of available templates for the site that you can choose from.

> **NOTE**
>
> If the template contains links (in or outside editable regions), paths will be automatically adjusted according to the location of the new page when it has been saved.

You can enter content only within editable regions in a page created from a template. Although you can type text or code into noneditable regions in Code view, Dreamweaver will automatically remove it when you save the file, switch to Design view, or preview the page in an external browser using the Preview command in Dreamweaver.

If you need to make changes to a page within noneditable regions, you have two options:

- Make the changes in the template itself, and then update the page as described in the next section of this chapter.
- Detach the page from the template using the Modify, Templates menu. If you detach the page from the template, noneditable regions are no longer enforced, and the page cannot be updated automatically to reflect changes in the template.

Updating Pages Created from Templates

After the .dwt file is created, you can reopen it for editing the same as you would an ordinary page. When you save your edits to the template, any pages already created from the template can be updated to reflect the changes in the template.

> **CAUTION**
> When you save changes to a template, be sure to use Save, not Save as Template. If you select Save as Template, Dreamweaver will treat the file as a new template, and its connection to all previously created pages will be broken.

Dreamweaver automatically prompts you to update pages created with a template when you save changes to it. A list of all pages is displayed, and you can choose to update all or some. If you choose not to update pages, you can still do so later using the Modify, Templates menu to update an individual page or all pages attached to a template.

> **CAUTION**
> Be careful updating pages if you have changed the editable regions in a template; you may lose content. Pages should be backed up before updating them with a template that has new or modified editable regions.

Summary

Templates provide a way of ensuring consistency in common code across pages, and they speed development by enabling you to start new pages with common code already in place. Dreamweaver templates have the additional advantages of enabling you to specify which regions of the template can be edited and to update pages when the template is modified. Templates can be created from any HTML page.

Sample Questions

1. How can you modify code or content in a noneditable region of a template? (Choose two.)
   A. Edit in Code view.
   B. Detach the page from the template.
   C. Edit the template and update the page.
   D. Save the page with a new filename.

2. How many templates can you define for a site?
   A. One
   B. Two
   C. One for each folder in the site
   D. As many as you want

CHAPTER 18

Server-side Includes

About Server-side Includes

As we've seen with frames, libraries, and templates, a common need in Web design and development is to use the same content over and over on different pages. Another way to solve this problem is server-side includes.

Server-side includes (SSI) instruct a server to insert another HTML file into the file currently being processed. SSI objects are executed when a user requests the file in a browser. Because of this, either file can change at any point, sometimes making maintenance on the site easier. It also means that there's nothing special to do to have your users see the effects of a changed SSI file. Simply update the file on the server and all future pages requests will include it.

SSI objects can be a bit tricky to set up and use, because they depend heavily on your deployment technology. Your server needs to be able to process them and may need to be configured with special settings or software. Usually your system administrator can tell you whether SSI can be used with your server and what you need to know to get them to work. Sometimes SSI objects will work only in pages that are identified with SHTML instead of HTM or HTML.

Creating the Server-side Include File

Before you can add an SSI to your page, you have to create the document that is to be included. This document will contain the segment of HTML code that will be inserted into the main document by the Web browser. Because this document is to be inserted into another document, it shouldn't contain any of the common HTML tags, such as <HEAD>, <TITLE>, <BODY>, and <HTML>. You want only the code that will be inserted.

To create a new file, use any of the methods you would normally use, such as File, New, or right-click in the Site window and choose New File. Highlight your new file and delete all the existing code in the Code view and add your new code. Frequently, this will be code cut out of the parent document. After you have this file created and saved, you're ready to add it to the parent document.

Adding a Server-side Include

SSI objects can be added to a page by clicking on or dragging the Server-Side Include object from the Common category of the Objects panel. You can also choose Insert, Server-Side Include from the menu. Either way, this will bring up a dialog box asking you to identify the file to be dynamically included. Identify the file and its path relationship to the current file. You can choose Document from the Relative To drop-down menu to create a path relative to the document itself, or choose Site Root to have the path remain relative to the site root.

> **TIP**
>
> It is a common convention to have all files that are to be included in this manner placed in a common folder called Includes off the site root, or within each major directory. This keeps down clutter, and it more clearly separates include files from normal HTML files.

After an SSI has been added, you can modify its properties by using the Properties Inspector. Simply select the inserted content and open the Properties Inspector. You'll notice that the content selects as a single block; it is not directly editable, because it is really being stored in a separate file.

The Properties Inspector will allow you to do the following:

- Manually alter the included filename.
- Choose a new file with the Select File dialog box.
- Launch the external file for editing.
- Alternate the type between Virtual and File.

Adding a Server-side Include Placeholder

Sometimes you will want to insert an SSI placeholder, in which you manually enter the filename or connect the file at a later time. This is common when the file is on the deployment server but has not been copied to your local development environment.

To insert a blank SSI placeholder, hold down the Ctrl key (or Option key on the Mac) and drag an SSI object to the Design view. You may then modify the object by selecting it and changing its properties in the Properties Inspector. If you know the path to the desired file on the server, you can manually type it into the Filename box.

File Versus Virtual Types

There are two modes for the inclusion of files: File and Virtual. Specifying File as the type is recommended when using Microsoft Internet Information Server. Specifying Virtual as the type is recommended when using the Apache Web Server. If you are not deploying using one of these technologies, see your documentation or ask your system administrator.

The difference between the two types of includes refers to how the Web server resolves the path to the desired file. In a File type, the path to include is based on the full path to the base file in the operating system. In a Virtual type, the path is based on the current Web server's root and does not include or rely on path information outside this base directory. Because File access in Microsoft Internet Information Server could in theory be used to cause security problems, the base installation of this server does not allow you to include files higher than the file containing the SSI object. If you need to include files at a higher level, see your system administrator, who will configure the system to allow such includes.

Code

Code for includes might look like the following:

```
<!-- #include virtual="/includes/menu.htm" -->
<!-- #include virtual="header.htm" -->
<!-- #include file="header.htm" -->
```

Notice that SSIs are simply a single reference to the file that you want to include. Because they are not standard HTML, they are bracketed inside an HTML comment, using `<!--` and `-->`. The `#include` is required to alert the system that an SSI is being performed. The designation "virtual" and "file" refers to the type of the include, which as you learned from the previous section is driven by the type of server being used for deployment. The file itself is included in quotes and, in the case of virtual servers, can consider the root path the same as the root of the Web server.

Testing

When an SSI is created in Macromedia Dreamweaver, the system loads the included file into the Design window at the appropriate location. When this happens, Dreamweaver is acting as if it is the Web server and does its best to resolve the path given to it and display the included information properly. Because of this, it is especially important to recognize that Dreamweaver has no way of knowing whether SSIs have been properly set up on your server or if they are even allowed. Seeing this technology work in the Design view is no substitute for seeing it work live on your deployment server. Whenever you plan to include SSI objects, you should verify with your systems administrator that they are allowed and, if possible, create some test pages to prove the point. Finding out in the last stages of deployment that the technology is not really available to your efforts is a sure way to cause extra work and frustration.

Advantages

SSIs have the following advantages:

- They allow you to centralize reused data in a single, easy-to-maintain file.
- They are relatively easy to implement, after you know they are available.
- They are included in the Design window, making it easy to see how they will be handled in your site.
- They allow reuse of content without having to worry if your user can support frames.
- Because copies of the information aren't stored inside your files, they keep your files smaller than when you use Templates or Library Items.

Disadvantages

SSIs also have some disadvantages, including the following:

- SSIs require you to know more about your deployment environment than you would need to know for typical HTML deployment.
- SSIs require more planning if you plan on moving the site to a different server.
- Dreamweaver's capability to preview SSI objects in the Design window sometimes leads developers into a false sense of security.
- SSIs execute after application server scripting languages, limiting the ability to use these languages in files that are to be included. Some languages, such as ColdFusion, have their own version of the statement to get around this problem.

> **NOTE**
>
> The capability of application servers to use their own version of the include statement, such as ColdFusion's `<CFINCLUDE>` statement, gives them a powerful edge in Web development. They do not depend on the Web server itself and can allow the included files to contain additional code. If you are planning to utilize an application server in your deployment, they are frequently the better way to go. If you plan to deploy without the aid of an application server, you'll be dependent on the SSI rules of your Web server.

Summary

SSIs are a powerful way to centralize information that will be used throughout your site. SSI files stay separate from the files that use them and are inserted by the Web server on request. Because SSI files are handled by the Web server and each Web server handles them slightly differently, care should be taken to assure that the technology is available for use when you decide to use it in your projects.

Sample Questions

1. SSIs can be of the following types (pick two):
   A. File
   B. Fixed
   C. Rotating
   D. Virtual
   E. Included

2. SSIs are used to:
   A. Update remote servers on a network
   B. Centralize common HTML in one place
   C. Push Java to a browser window
   D. Store information in a database

CHAPTER 19

Using Behaviors

About Behaviors

Behaviors enable you to add interactions to your Web pages beyond the typical capabilities of HTML. Dreamweaver has an entire selection of behaviors built-in and also can have behaviors plugged in to it to allow additional functionality.

Although behaviors are a Macromedia Dreamweaver–specific concept, they are created using a standard Web browser technology—JavaScript. Working on the behavior level rather than the JavaScript level allows you to more quickly and easily apply and manipulate interactions on your Web pages, without having to worry about the specifics of JavaScript coding. With each behavior, Dreamweaver generates a graphical interface, which allows you to set and manipulate properties of the behavior.

To use a behavior, you will need to become familiar with three parts. All uses of a behavior have these parts, and you will need to consider each part to appropriately use behaviors. They are the following:

- Objects
- Actions
- Events

Objects

Objects are the items to which the behavior is applied. This is usually what the user will interact with in some manner, such as clicking. Before you can add a behavior to the page, you have to figure out what object you want to apply the behavior to. You do this by clicking the object. If you do not click any object, the behavior will be applied to the default object—the page. As we'll discuss, not all behaviors can be applied to all objects.

Actions

The action is the part of the behavior that describes what is to happen. Actions are determined by what level of compatibility is selected and what behaviors are currently installed on the system. Actions have properties that allow them to be customized. For instance, an action that moves the user to a new URL will have a property specifying the URL that the user should be moved to and into which window or frames the URL should be loaded.

Events

An event specifies a trigger for the action and is applied to the object. In a sense, events tie together these two parts to make a whole. An event, such as onClick, specifies that when the object is clicked by the mouse, the related action should be launched. Events change depending on the object selected and the level of browser compliance. A button, for instance, can have an onClick event attached to it, whereas a page may have an onLoad event attached to its `<body>` tag. Events are related directly to event handlers, which are predetermined keywords that specify what events different objects are able to see and react to.

Applying Behaviors

The first things you need to do when you want to add a behavior to your page is to identify the object that it is to be applied to, the action that is to happen, and the event that is to be used to trigger the action.

After you have identified these three elements, you are ready to apply the behavior to the page. Start by selecting the object to which you want to apply the behavior. To select the page itself, simply place the cursor in an area in which it doesn't select a specific item on the page.

Next, open the Behaviors panel by selecting Window, Behaviors. The Behaviors panel allows you to add, remove, and alter behaviors on the objects of your page. To add the behavior to the selected object, click the "+" pull-down menu. This opens a set of behaviors that can be applied to the object you currently have selected at the browser level you are currently using.

> **NOTE**
>
> If you expected an item to be available and find at this point that it is not, there are two common explanations. Either the behavior you are looking for cannot be applied to the object you have selected, or you are currently targeting a browser level that does not support the behavior you want to apply. To remedy the first problem, try selecting a different object on the page, or try selecting no object at all to select the page level. To solve the second problem, click the "+" button to

> reveal the pull-down menu, and choose the Show Events For submenu. You can choose a browser level that is more up-to-date than the one currently selected to enable more behaviors.

After you select the desired behavior, Dreamweaver will ask you to set up the behavior with a dialog box. Each behavior has a different dialog box that allows you to customize how the behavior works in that specific case. Notice that each item on a page that has the same behavior applied to it can have different settings for the behavior. When you are finished, click OK. If you have to fill out a required field that is needed to make the behavior work, you will be notified at this point and you will not be able to close the dialog box until you fill out the required fields.

After the dialog box is closed, you will find that the Behaviors panel contains an entry with both an event and an action. Usually, the event is not the event that you want to use with this behavior. To change the event, use the pull-down menu by clicking the down arrow next to the event name. Events, like behaviors, are specific to the browser that you are targeting and the current object that you have selected. If the event you want to use is not available, you can either use a different event or change the target browser level. If the event is still not listed, you may have selected an object that cannot be used with your desired event.

Multiple behaviors can be applied to the same object. Additionally, these behaviors can use either the same events or separate events.

Removing Behaviors

Behaviors can be removed from objects by using the Behaviors panel. To remove an object, select the object from which you want to remove behaviors. If the Behaviors panel is not already open, open it. Select the behavior that you want to remove and click the "–" button. If you do not have a behavior selected, the "–" button will be unavailable.

Behavior Order

When multiple behaviors are applied to an object using the same event, order sometimes becomes important. For instance, if you are using a pop-up message to tell users they are about to leave your site, and you are using a behavior to jump to a new URL immediately following their approval, the order you use to set up the behaviors is very important. To change the order of the actions applied to an object, select the action that you want to move and click either the up arrow or the down arrow in the Behaviors panel. This moves the action in front of the other actions using that event, or behind them. If no other actions are using the same event, or if the action is already first or last, one or both of the arrows will be disabled.

Target Browser Levels

The target browser level determines the behaviors available to you, as well as the events that can be selected for each behavior on the page. You can reset the target browser level by changing the Show Events For menu to a new option. In turn, this affects both the Events menu and the Actions menu by changing the options available on each. Both the Behaviors and the Events menus change to allow only the events that can be used with the specific browser.

Choosing a target browser level should come from an understanding of the target audience and the technology that they are likely to have installed. You should not alter the target browser simply because it's the easier way to accomplish a goal, without considering the impact on the target audience. In most cases, the earlier the browser, as determined by version number, the fewer events and behaviors you'll be able to use. Choosing both browsers at a particular version level, such as 4.0 and Later Browsers will cause even fewer events and behaviors to appear. This is because any behavior or event that doesn't work in both browsers will be omitted from the list.

Available options for targeting browsers:

- 3.0 and Later Browsers
- 4.0 and Later Browsers
- IE 3.0
- IE 4.0
- IE 5.0
- Netscape 3.0
- Netscape 4.0
- Netscape 6.0

Although changing your target browser in mid-development changes the options available to you, it doesn't do anything to code already developed on your page or on your site. If you find yourself in this position, you should consider running the Check Target Browsers utility to flag pages for which you may be using unsupported events.

Behaviors in (Parentheses)

Some behaviors in the menu are listed in parentheses. These are used for adding a behavior to the link (`<a>` tag) around an object, rather than to the object itself. If no link is present, one is created. When Dreamweaver adds an `<a>` tag, it puts in a null script as the link so that all browsers will recognize the link and perform a cursor change over it. A null link is a short JavaScript statement that does no action. The script used is `"javascript:;"`. In this case the term "javascript" and the colon tell the browser that a single line of JavaScript is to be executed, and the semicolon ends the line without performing any action.

JavaScript and Behaviors

When a behavior is applied to an object in a page, two pieces of JavaScript are added to the page. The first part is inside the `<head>` tag. This section of code provides the routine (or routines) needed on the page to perform the behavior. Simple behaviors will have just a single, simple routine, but more complex behaviors will require a main routine and then additional helper routines. When several behaviors are added to a document, they will share helper routines rather than inserting multiple copies of the same code.

The second piece of JavaScript that is added is inserted into the tag related to the object in which the behavior is being applied. This includes the JavaScript event handler that describes the trigger event. It also includes a call to the actions that have been applied to that object. Each action calls the appropriate routine in the <head> tag until all routines have been called. Within each call is a list of the parameters used to customize the behavior for that use. These are what you set when you modify the behavior through the dialog box. This is also why each use of the behavior on a page can have different settings; they are stored within the tag attached to each object, rather than in the common JavaScript routine in the <head> tag.

A simple use of a behavior in a page may look like the following:

```
<html>
<head>
<title>Behaviors</title>

<script language="JavaScript">
<!--
function MM_popupMsg(msg) { //v1.0
    alert(msg);
}
//-->
</script>
</head>
<body bgcolor="#FFFFFF" test="#000000" onLoad="MM_popupMsg('Hello World!')">
<h2>Behaviors</h2>
</body>
</html>
```

This code is the result of adding a Popup Message behavior to a page and configuring it to display the text “Hello World!.” Notice how the common routine is centralized at the top of the page and how the specific setting, in this case the text, is included in the JavaScript attached to the onLoad attribute of the Body tag. This code, when executed, will cause the “Hello World!” pop-up to appear when the page is loaded by a browser.

Because behaviors are created entirely out of JavaScript code, the browser executes them just like JavaScript that you may have created or copied from another source. No plug-ins or server extensions are required to run your pages. Also, you can create your own behaviors or add additional behaviors to your installation of Dreamweaver by downloading them from the Macromedia.com Web site.

NOTE

Behaviors are written in and implemented using JavaScript. Frequently, people confuse the two distinct technologies, Java and JavaScript, or think that they are one. This is becoming even more of an issue now that Microsoft has discontinued its distribution of Java with Internet Explorer 6.0. JavaScript, however, is built directly into the browser and is supported both by Microsoft and Netscape.

TIP

To learn how to create your own Dreamweaver behaviors, see the help guide titled Extending Dreamweaver under the Help menu.

Commonly Used Behaviors

The following are the most commonly used behaviors in Dreamweaver. You should become familiar with their uses and functions.

Check Browser

This behavior allows you to segregate your users based on browser level. This enables you to develop a more advanced Web site for high-end users and provide the same information in more universally formatted HTML pages.

The behavior allows you to set a desired version level for Netscape Navigator and Internet Explorer and allows you to specify what should happen to users who use a different browser, such as Opera or Web TV. Users who pass (or don't pass) the test can be sent to one URL, to an alternate URL, or can be kept on the current page. The behavior can be used on page entry (onLoad) or after a user has clicked an option (onClick).

Go to URL

This behavior, in its simplest form, works like a normal <a> tag in that it creates a link to a page that can be loaded in the default location or targeted to a specific frame on the window. It is more powerful than a normal link, however, because it can be triggered by any valid event and because it can load multiple pages into multiple frames—all within a single use.

Open Browser Window

This behavior opens a designated page into a new browser window of specific dimensions. It allows you to specifically set attributes of the new window, such as the existence of a Navigation toolbar, a Location toolbar, a menu bar, a status bar, and scrollbars. You can also specify whether the window can be resized by the user.

Swap Image

The Swap Image behavior is commonly referred to as the Rollover behavior because of its most common use, which is to create rollover effects for buttons. This behavior swaps a secondary image for an image on the Web page when a specific event is seen, usually onMouseOver. This behavior also adds a second behavior to restore the image with the onMouseOut event and causes the secondary image to be preloaded to increase performance.

To use this behavior on an image, the related `<img>` tag must have a name attribute, which should not change after the behavior is applied. Also, the image that swaps out does not have to be the image receiving the event. A larger image, for instance, could be swapped out to highlight different parts of a diagram, depending on the option selected.

Hide/Show Layers

This behavior is used to hide or show one or more layers in a file. This behavior is typically used to create layer-driven pull-down menus or to display multiple parts of an HTML file at one time. This behavior cannot be used unless layers already exist in the document.

Commonly Used Events

The following are the most commonly used events in behavior use.

onClick/onMouseDown

These events are used to detect user mouse clicks.

onLoad/onUnload

These events are used to trigger an event either after the page is finished loading (that is, all graphics have been requested and received) or before a page is left. For the first, no user interaction is required; the system sends itself this message when it recognizes that the loading process is complete. For the latter, the system sends this message to itself whenever an action is about to cause a new URL to load in the browser window.

onMouseOver/onMouseOut

These events are used to trigger rollovers for graphical buttons. They also are sometimes used to provide additional details about a button in the status bar.

Summary

Behaviors allow additional functionality that goes beyond the capabilities of HTML to be added to a page. Behaviors are created in JavaScript and require an understanding of the target object, event, and action desired. Behaviors are added and manipulated through the Behaviors panel, which adds JavaScript routines to the `<HEAD>` tag and adds event handlers to the related objects in the `<BODY>` section.

Sample Questions

1. The Show Events For menu allows you to:
   A. Change the target browser level
   B. Add your own events to the Event menu
   C. Test your code for compliance with various browsers
   D. Add a behavior to an object
2. Which pair of events is commonly used to create rollovers?
   A. `onLoad/onUnload`
   B. `onMouseOver/onMouseOut`
   C. `onClick/onMouseDown`
   D. `Swap Image/Swap Image Restore`
3. Behaviors are implemented in what language?
   A. HTML
   B. Visual Basic
   C. JavaScript
   D. C++

CHAPTER 20

Team Collaboration

Macromedia's Dreamweaver is an excellent tool for building Web sites, whether it's a single developer with a small Web site or many developers building a large site.

Dreamweaver has built-in features to enable team collaboration. These features include

- Effective use of comments for documenting within HTML pages
- Use of design notes for self-documenting decisions and changes within files
- Capability to lock files when in use so others can know which files are available using check in and check out

Commenting Files

You can comment your code in Dreamweaver to enable you to maintain the documents and track the changes you make. Dreamweaver classifies comments as an invisible object, so you can insert them by choosing Insert, Invisible Tags, Comment or by using the Invisibles Object panel's Insert Comment icon.

After comments are created, a visual indicator is put into the Document window's Design view.

> **TIP**
>
> To comment out a section of text or code, select it, copy it to the Clipboard, and then insert the comment. Paste the copied text or code into the Comment dialog box.

Creating a comment creates the HTML comment tag, an example of which is shown next:

```
<!--comment text -->
```

CAUTION

Comments are stored as HTML and are therefore sent to the browser. So beware of using them for any private information.

Design Notes

Instead of leaving comments about version numbers, due dates, and other tracking information within your file, create design notes for your pages. A design note is a hidden text file that stores information about another file; they are not included within the file and are therefore not visible to Web site users.

TIP

You can use design notes not only with Web pages, but also with images, multimedia files, and any other files in your local site.

Enabling and Creating Design Notes

Enable design notes for each site using the Site Definition dialog box obtained by clicking Site, Define Sites, and then picking the desired site.

After you enable design notes, you can add design notes to any page in the site from either the Site window or the Document window using File, Design Notes.

Table 20.1 shows the options and possible values for the design notes information on the Basic Info tab:

Table 20.1 Design Notes Information

Option	Value
File	Noneditable name of the file to which you assign design notes
Location	Physical path to the file
Status	Set the status of the file to one of the following values: • Draft • Revision1 • Revision2 • Revision3 • Alpha • Beta • Final • Needs attention
Date icon	Stamp the date of the note
Notes	Free text notes of the revision
Show When File Is Opened	Check this box if you want Dreamweaver to pop open the design notes whenever the file is opened.

> **CAUTION**
>
> You will not be able to add design notes to read-only files. Dreamweaver needs to write a comment to the file, so it must be write enabled.

You can set up Dreamweaver to use a common set of design notes for each file in a set of name/value pairs. This is done on the All Info tab of the Design Notes dialog box. This dialog box enables you to create a standard set of notes.

You can access design notes through the Notes icon that appears in the Site window next to each page that has notes.

Storage Location

The first time you create a design note, Dreamweaver creates a _notes directory within the current directory. Each design note is named for its file, plus an additional extension (.mno—Macromedia Note).

Notes Clean Up

Dreamweaver does not remove design notes from the directory when the associated file is deleted. To clean up orphaned design notes, use the Clean Up button under the Design Notes category in the site definition window.

> **TIP**
>
> If you disable design notes for an entire site, Dreamweaver will prompt you to remove all design notes. In this way, you can remove design notes for an entire site.

Check In/Out

Dreamweaver can enable collaboration in a team environment with a shared set of files through the use of check in and check out. When a developer has a file checked out, it displays as checked out in the Site window, with the name of the developer for all to see. By knowing who is currently working on a file, developers can avoid working on the same files at the same time. When the file is checked back in, the checked-out user information is cleared and the file becomes available.

> **NOTE**
>
> Do not confuse Dreamweaver's check in/out functionality with those of a full source-control system, such as Microsoft's SourceSafe server product. For instance, Dreamweaver cannot roll back to any change made to a file. It is used for collaboration so only one developer can modify a file at a time.

Enabling and Using Check In/Out

Check in and check out must be enabled using the Site Definition window, found under Site, Define Sites, and by choosing a site to enable. Check in/out is enabled using the

Remote Site category, so a remote site must be set up before enabling. Other settings in the Site Definition window for check in/out are the following:

- Check Out Name—Each user inputs his or her name so other developers know who is checking out the files.
- E-mail Address—User's e-mail address, so developers can automatically e-mail the person who has the file checked out.

When you check out a file from a remote site, Dreamweaver retrieves the most recent version of that file from the server. When Dreamweaver gets the file, it overwrites any copy that might be on your local drive. Dreamweaver will then use your check in/out name in the Site window for all other developers to see and will not allow other users to check out that file. If you specified an e-mail address, your check-out name becomes a link that launches an e-mail message to you.

NOTE

Dreamweaver enables check out by writing another file with a .lck extension when a file is checked out. It cleans up this file when the file is checked back in.

When you check in a file, it transfers the file back to the remote server and clears your name from the checked out column in the Site window. Your local copy of the file is then switched to read-only.

CAUTION

Dreamweaver allows you to override a checked-out file, and you can change the read-only attribute of a file and modify it. Developers should be instructed not to circumvent these safeguards.

Summary

Macromedia Dreamweaver enables team collaboration and edit tracking using simple comments, enhanced design notes, and the capability to single-thread modifications to Web site files. Comments are inserted into the document as HTML, whereas design notes are stored in separate files so they are kept private. Checked out files are displayed as such in the Site window, so many developers can know who has a file out and can wait for it to be checked back in.

Sample Questions

1. Design notes are stored inside an HTML document and therefore are viewable by browsers.
   A. True
   B. False
2. Dreamweaver's check in/out feature enables developers to revert a file to a previous state.
   A. True
   B. False

PART IV

TESTING AND DEPLOYMENT

CHAPTER 21

Testing Web Sites

Introduction

Comprehensive testing is crucial to the success of a Web site, and far too often, testing is inadequate. Following are some of the common user experiences that attest to that inadequacy:

- HTTP 404 (page not found) errors
- Missing images with no alternative text to indicate what information the images contained or linked to
- Dead-end pages that contain no links
- Obsolete pages, or pages that were never intended to be viewed, found through search engines

In most cases, such site problems result from minor code errors that can be easily fixed—if anyone catches them before the site goes live.

Fortunately, Dreamweaver has sophisticated tools for site testing (along with tools, such as automatic link updating, that prevent many errors before they happen). This chapter reviews the site-testing tools available in Dreamweaver.

Checking Links

As long as you work within Dreamweaver sites, links within your sites should never get broken. Whenever you move a file in the Site window, Dreamweaver checks for links that will be broken by the move and repairs them, unless you explicitly ask that they not be fixed. Changes in file structure made outside of Dreamweaver may still result in broken links, however.

Links to pages outside the site pose more of a problem, not because they change based on anything you do, but because they change without notice.

You can check links in Dreamweaver sitewide or for selected files and folders. Link checks are accessed through the Site menu or the right-click pop-up menu for individual or selected files. The link check generates a report of bad links, and you can double-click these to open the pages for editing at the point of the broken link.

> **CAUTION**
>
> Dreamweaver does not test the validity of `mailto` links or `hrefs` that point to JavaScript commands, even to check for the existence of a called function.

The broken links report also includes a note on orphaned files—files that cannot be reached through any links.

> **TIP**
>
> Pay attention to the orphaned files note. Sometimes, good reasons exist to keep files with a site, even though you do not intend them to be viewed by users, but orphans are often created accidentally by developers forgetting to add links from other pages. Also, orphaned files may contain notes or other information used in development but that are not intended to be part of the finished site. In some cases the orphaned files may contain sensitive information, and users may stumble across these files by accident or through search engines.

Site Reports

In addition to checking links, Dreamweaver can generate several useful reports on your site through the Site, Reports menu. The reports are divided into two groups, Workflow and HTML, which are described in Tables 21.1 and 21.2, respectively.

Table 21.1 Dreamweaver Workflow Reports

Report	Description
Checked Out By	Shows files that are checked out, grouped by the development team member who checked out the document. This check is crucial to ensuring that the latest version of all files is checked in before the site goes live. It is also useful to run this report during development to ensure that team members are checking in files regularly to minimize the risk of lost work because of system failures.
Design Notes	Shows any files that have design notes attached to them. This report should be run to ensure that no design notes for needed revisions or additions to files have been forgotten.

Table 21.2 Dreamweaver HTML Reports

Report	Description
Combinable Nested Font Tags	Shows instances of nested `<font>` tags that could be combined to make your code simpler and more efficient.
Missing Alt Text	Shows instances of `<img>` tags where no alt text has been provided. Alt text is required for accessibility and is good practice in all cases.
Redundant Nested Tags	Shows instances in which nested tags perform redundant functions and clutter your code unnecessarily.
Removable Empty Tags	Shows instances of tags with no content that can be removed to clean up your code.
Untitled Documents	Shows any pages that have no titles; titles are important to improve the chances of search engines correctly identifying the page contents.

TIP

It is a good idea to run the HTML reports often and clean up problems that are found. Code clutter builds up as you repeatedly edit files; it makes your pages unnecessarily large and your code difficult to read.

Browser Sizing

The normal and maximized sizes of a browser window depend on the resolution of the display on the user's system. In the early days of GUI browsers, most monitors and video drivers supported only 640×480 pixel resolution, and a few supported 800×600 pixels.

The situation is very different and more challenging for Web developers now. On computer monitors, resolutions up to 1280×1024 pixels are not uncommon, and even higher resolutions are supported in some cases. On the other hand, Web-enabled devices, such as PDAs and handheld phones, may have resolutions considerably smaller than 640×480 pixels, which at one time was considered the least common denominator.

Fortunately, Dreamweaver enables you to resize the Document window to match screen sizes for different resolutions. The available resolutions can be set in the Dreamweaver Preferences, but the most common ones are set up in advance.

To change the window size (in Design View only), you click the resolution setting in the window status bar to open a drop-down menu of available resolutions and choose the one you want. By choosing various settings, you can get an idea of how the contents of a page will scale to different resolutions.

TIP

You do not need to wait for the site-testing phase to take advantage of the Document window sizing feature. Setting the window size to match your target display resolution will help you fit content appropriately as you lay out pages and develop content.

Also, remember that the Document window doesn't give you a true picture of the page as it will be rendered by a browser. You can also size a browser window to emulate different display resolutions. To help you size the window, use Fireworks to create rectangles of different dimensions—640×480, 800×600, and so forth—and put these on your desktop as wallpaper to help you size the browser window.

Download Time Testing

One of the crucial aspects of site usability is the download time for pages, especially pages that serve as the front door to the site. The biggest factor in download time—aside from network traffic, which you have no control over—is media files, and the majority of media files are images.

The status bar of the Dreamweaver Document window displays the total weight of the current page and the approximate download time at a specified connection speed. You can modify the connection speed used to calculate download time in the Dreamweaver Preferences. No hard rule exists as to the maximum tolerable download time, but given the wealth of sites users have to choose from, you cannot reasonably expect them to wait for more than 10 or 15 seconds for a page to load, unless they have good reason to believe that the information is worth waiting for.

TIP

Probably the most effective way of reducing page weight is to optimize image files. Many image files can be reduced by 50% or more without serious loss of image quality. Macromedia Fireworks has excellent image-optimization tools for all image formats, providing you with previews so that you see how much image quality will be sacrificed.

When even optimized images are large, put them on pages inside the site and try to cache them on the user's system before they are viewed. To do this, put an `<img>` tag pointing to the large image at the very end of the body on pages users are likely to pass through before they get to the image. Set the image height and width to 1 on pages you use to cache the image, so that it will be invisible but will still download.

Summary

Dreamweaver provides a number of site-testing tools to help you ensure that your site functions flawlessly when it goes live. You can test links sitewide or for selected pages, and you can generate reports on such items as forgotten design notes and empty or redundant tags that clutter your code and make pages larger. Dreamweaver also has tools to help you fit content to various screen resolutions and identify pages that will take an excessive amount of time to download.

Sample Questions

1. Which of the following will not be flagged by the Dreamweaver link checker?
   A. A full URL pointing to a server that is down for maintenance
   B. A partial URL with a path relative to the current location
   C. A partial URL with a path relative to the Web document root
   D. A call to a nonexistent JavaScript function

2. What is an orphaned file?
   A. A file located outside the site directory tree
   B. An HTML file that is missing a `<head>` tag
   C. A file to which there are no links from other pages
   D. A file that failed to upload to the remote site

CHAPTER 22

Transferring Files to Remote Servers

About File Transfers in Dreamweaver

Dreamweaver uses built-in tools to move your site from the local development station to remote servers where it can be tested or deployed. The same tools can be used to move a site from a remote server back to a local station, either as part or all of a site. These tools can also be used to synchronize local and remote sites, transferring only files that have changed or deleting files that have been removed from the local site.

Dreamweaver's capabilities for transferring files depend largely on how preferences on the station and settings related to the site are configured. Dreamweaver can hook into a variety of Web-based protocols, including FTP and WebDav, and can use check-in/check-out features to assist with version control issues.

After your files are loaded into production, Dreamweaver's extended Find and Replace features can help you make broad changes to your pages, which can then be resubmitted into production.

Site Preferences

The most general preferences that affect how your sites can interface with remote servers are found in the Site Preferences panel. Open the Preferences panel using Edit, Preferences, and then switch to the Site category.

> **NOTE**
>
> It is assumed that these preferences would stay the same across all your sites. If this is not always true, you may find yourself switching some of these settings when editing different sites.

This panel enables you to customize the following:

- Local File or Remote File Positioning—Sets positioning for the Site Files window to show local or remote files either on the right or the left.
- Dependent Files Prompting—Controls whether Dreamweaver prompts you to download dependent files when you put or get files.
- FTP Connection Settings—Controls how long FTP connections are open and what the timeout is when waiting for a response from the server.
- Firewall Settings—Sets the firewall address and port. You can choose whether to use this firewall in each of your sites.
- Save Files Before Putting—Forces files to be saved before putting them to the server.

Remote Site Definition

Each site has a group of settings that is alterable for each individual site. To access these settings, open the Site Definition dialog box for the specific site. In the Site Definition dialog box, change the category to Remote Info. By default, the Server Access model will be set to None, meaning that no information exists about any remote deployment of these files.

Changing the setting to another access model allows various settings to be set. The other access models follow.

FTP

File Transfer Protocol (FTP) is the standard file transfer method on the Web for moving files from one server to another. This protocol enables you to set the following:

- FTP Host—The Web address of the FTP server to which you are connecting.
- Host Directory—The directory within the server that matches the directory of the Local Root folder. You should never add "ftp://" to the hostname.
- Login—The FTP server login.
- Password—The FTP server password for the specified login. Optionally, you can save the password with the site settings.
- Use Passive FTP—For use with firewalls. Allows the local software to set up the FTP connection instead of the remote server.
- Use Firewall—Connects using the firewall set in the Preferences panel.
- Enable File Check In and Check Out—Enables check-in and check-out services for the site.
- Check Out Files When Opening—Makes you the owner when you open files from the remote site.

- Check Out Name—The name under which you are checking out files. Should be unique for every user and station that is accessing the site.
- E-mail Address—Stored when files are checked out. Should be the valid e-mail address of the user.

> **NOTE**
>
> The directory specified in your local settings and the directory specified as the Host Directory, must structurally refer to the same directory. If they do not, your get, put, and synchronize actions will cause havoc on your files and file server. Sometimes the login and password tell the server to start at a particular path that matches the Local Root folder, which saves the trouble of having to find the path to the server. In some cases, you need to enter a slash ("/") as the Host Directory to let the server know that you are starting in the default directory.

Local/Network

This enables you to move files to the server either onto a local drive of your development platform or to a drive that is accessible across the network without use of Internet protocols.

The following options are available to you when accessing the server with this method:

- Remote Folder—A file-based path to the remote server root. This can be set by typing or by using the File dialog box. Similar to Host Directory when using FTP, this must point to the remote root directory.
- Refresh Remote File List Automatically—Allows the remote file list to update more frequently.
- Enable File Check In and Check Out—Enables check-in and check-out services for the site.
- Check Out Files When Opening—Makes you the owner when you open files from the remote site.
- Check Out Name—The name under which you are checking out files. Should be unique for every user and station that is accessing the site.
- E-mail Address—Stored when files are checked out. Should be the valid e-mail address of the user.

SourceSafe

SourceSafe enables you to use your SourceSafe client to store and access sites. SourceSafe has advanced version control and management capabilities built in. On the Windows platform, Dreamweaver uses the Microsoft Visual SourceSafe client, and on the Macintosh it uses the Metrowerks Visual SourceSafe client.

Settings for SourceSafe access are stored in a Settings dialog box, accessible by clicking the Settings button:

- Database Path—The file path to the SourceSafe database.
- Project—The Project directory in the database.

- Username—Your username in the SourceSafe system.
- Password—Your password in the SourceSafe system. Optionally, you can save your password with the site settings.

WebDAV

WebDAV allows remote Web management of files in a controlled fashion.

Settings for WebDAV access are stored in a Settings dialog box, accessible by clicking the Settings button:

- URL—The Web path to the remote root directory.
- Username—Your username in the WebDAV system.
- Password—Your password in the WebDAV system. Optionally, you can save your password with the site settings.
- E-mail—Should be your valid e-mail address.

Site Window

The Site window drives the transfer of files between the local and remote sites. An arrow at the bottom of the window allows the remote files to be shown and hidden from view. When a site is properly configured, the structure of the remote site should match the structure of the local site.

Connecting and Showing Files

Connecting to the remote site is done by selecting the appropriate site in the Site pull-down list and clicking the Connect button. If the Connect button is grayed out, no remote site has been established. If the button shows a black circle with disconnected sockets, you are not connected. If the button shows connected sockets and a green circle, you are currently connected to the site. Files will be shown automatically in the remote files panel. If you need to refresh the files in either panel, click the Refresh button at the right of the Connect button.

Put

The `put` command is used after selecting a file, folders, or group of files and folders in the local site. It uploads the files and folders to the relative location in the remote site. Depending on the preferences, you may be asked if dependent files should be uploaded to the remote server.

Get

The `get` command is used after selecting a file, folders, or groups of files and folders in the remote site. It downloads files to the local site in the appropriate location. Depending on the preferences, you may be asked if dependent files should be downloaded from the server.

Dependent Files

Dependent files are files that are used directly by the parent file. They include graphics, videos, and files used in server-side includes. They do not include library items or templates. Depending on your settings, Dreamweaver will ask whether you want to move dependent files with the files you are getting or putting. Not downloading dependent files can speed up the transmission but can make editing and previewing the file difficult.

Synchronize

Synchronize is an advanced method of getting and putting files. To start a synchronization, select Site, Synchronize. This displays the Synchronize Files dialog box, which contains the following options:

- Synchronize—Specifies the entire site or specific files selected remotely or locally.
- Direction—Specifies what to do with newer files. You can put only, get only, or both get and put based on date.
- Delete Remote Files Not on Local Drive—Allows remote files that are not found locally to be deleted. Used to clean up old files that have been rearranged locally between synchronizations.

After setting the correct options, click the Preview button, which generates a list of all files to be uploaded, downloaded, or deleted. After unchecking any actions you do not want to perform, you can click the OK button to finish the synchronization.

Check In/Out

Check In and Check Out enable the files to be marked as "in use" by a specific user. The method used for marking the file changes with the remote access method. For local/network access or FTP access, simple .lck files are added into the directory that holds the status of any given file. When this feature is enabled, you will see green checks next to files that you have checked out and red checks next to files checked out by others. Also, two other buttons appear in the interface: one used to check out files and the other to check in files. Files that are checked back in remain on your local site but are marked with a lock. This shows that although you can preview and use the file locally, you should not make changes to the file, because it may be checked out by others.

Locally Moving and Renaming Files (Drag Around)

When you rearrange or rename files and folders in the site window, Dreamweaver will attempt to update related paths and links to the affected files. When this happens, you should be conscious of several things. One is that to make changes to update files, you may have to check them out. If you are unable to check them out because someone else has them checked out already, you will have broken links in your files that you will have to go back later and fix. Another thing to keep in mind is that the old files with the old names will still exist on the server. To clean up this problem, you can use the Delete Remote Files option in the Synchronization feature.

Design Notes

Design notes can be uploaded and shared with the team. Notes can be added to any file in the site, including HTML files, graphical files, movies, templates, and the like. To make sure the team can see your notes, you should enable the Upload Design Notes for Sharing feature. This is found in the Site Definition window, in the Design Notes category.

Find and Replace

Dreamweaver has powerful Find and Replace features to help you maintain your site and modify it to reflect new content, designs, or changes in Web technology.

Using the Edit, Find and Replace dialog box from the Document or Site window enables you to find and/or replace within

- The current document
- The entire site
- Multiple files in the site
- Selected files within folders

Most word processing programs have robust find and replace mechanisms, but Dreamweaver is specific to HTML development and therefore has great find methods, such as searching for the following:

- Source Code—Lets you search for specific text strings in the HTML source code
- Text—Lets you search for specific text strings in the Document window
- Text (Advanced)—Lets you search for specific text strings that are either within or not within a tag or tags
- Specific Tag—Lets you search for specific tags, attributes, and attribute values

> **TIP**
>
> Search for an actual return character by pressing Ctrl+Enter or Shift+Enter (Windows) or Ctrl+Return, Shift+Return, or Command+Return (Macintosh) when specifying the search string. Deselect the Ignore Whitespace Differences option when performing this search if you're not using regular expressions.

Dreamweaver also enables you to use Regular Expressions in your search. Regular Expressions let you specify a pattern of text without specifying the exact text. For instance, a social security number has a distinct pattern of *nnn-nn-nnnn*, where the *n* represents numbers specific to each American's social security number.

The Use Regular Expressions option causes certain characters and short strings (such as ?, *, \w, and \b) in your search string to be interpreted as regular expression operators. For example, a search for "...-..-...." will match any social security number pattern found in the documents selected. This can be applied to other operators for beginning of line, end of line, and so on. This is a very powerful, yet somewhat complicated, feature in searches.

Dreamweaver also enables you to store your searches so that you can apply them later.

Summary

Dreamweaver allows multiple methods of access to your deployment server, including FTP, WebDAV, SourceSafe, and Local/Network. Remote access features can use check in and check out features built in to Dreamweaver or can use the check in and check out features built in to the specified access method.

When Dreamweaver gets and puts files, it establishes the local and remote paths, based on what it knows about each location. When you move or rename files or folders remotely, Dreamweaver will update and, if it needs to, check out each affected file.

Synchronization allows newer files to be uploaded and/or downloaded between the local and remote locations. It also allows extra files to be removed on the remote site that do not exist on the local site.

Changes can be made to your global site or down to a specific page using Dreamweaver's extended find and replace options. Regular Expressions, which provide powerful matching capabilities, are supported in searches. Specific tags and attributes associated with them can be found and modified quickly and easily.

Sample Questions

1. Check In and Check Out buttons are available only when:
   A. The site allows check in and check out.
   B. WebDAV and SourceSafe are being used.
   C. The remote site is being connected to.
   D. The remote site is a Unix platform.

2. For Dreamweaver to properly put and get files with FTP, what two things must structurally match?
   A. Site name and FTP host.
   B. The location of the remote and local Templates folders.
   C. The FTP host and the Firewall host.
   D. The Local Root folder and the Host Directory.

3. Design notes can be automatically shared.
   A. True
   B. False

PART V

APPENDIX

APPENDIX A

Answers

1

1. D. A URL provides an address for single file.
2. B. DHTML is a term used to describe dynamic manipulation of documents on the client, but is not covered by any specification.

2

1. A. Style sheets are not included in the Assets panel.
2. C. The Quick Tag Editor provides code hints to help you choose correct tags and attributes.

3

1. B and C. You can map to a network drive and have Dreamweaver copy over the files, or you can use FTP to put the files on the remote server.
2. A. You cannot use Dreamweaver as true source control for rolling back files.

4

1. A. "You would consider all of these factors." Each of these factors is a valid piece of information that would later help you decide how to design your navigation and content.
2. A. False. It's usually a good idea to consider the navigation of the larger site when designing a smaller site within it. Generating your own look and feel can confuse users and slow them down.

3. A. Leave. E-commerce site users need help identifying products that will help solve their problems, and need quick and easy methods to process the sale. If they run into trouble somewhere in the process, they will usually leave and never return.

5

1. C. The others are all valid `<META>` tags, however.
2. A and B. Netscape only uses the `Width` and `Height` attributes for page margins.
3. A. The left margin attribute is set inside the `<body>` tag.

6

1. B. This CSS property controls which element appears on top when elements overlap.
2. C. Dreamweaver will not allow you to convert layers to a table if there are overlapping layers.

7

1. B. Delimited text format. Dreamweaver can import data from this format. Delimited text field files can be created from most database and spreadsheet programs.
2. A. Hidden spacer graphics. Hidden spacer graphics help keep cells sized correctly, and are important to remember when using autostretching.

8

1. B. Clicking the current justification removes all justification information. Clicking Left Justify does not remove the attribute; it just alters it.
2. B. The color of text is stored in the `<font>` tag inside the color attribute.
3. D. HTML styles are stored in the site's Library directory in a file called `styles.xml`.

9

1. B and C. The `hspace` and `vspace` attributes define horizontal and vertical whitespace around the image.
2. B. Because it supports an unlimited number of colors, the JPEG format is usually the best choice for photographic images; PNG also supports unlimited colors but is not as widely supported by browsers.

10

1. B. The # sign is required to indicate a named anchor; C is incorrect because the name is case sensitive.
2. B and D. B uses the correct predefined target to open a new window via HTML; D uses the correct syntax to open a new window via JavaScript.

11

1. B. If you were to copy and paste information into Dreamweaver, it will not format it into tabular format—it will only format it using <p> tags. Importing a delimited file will automatically format tabular data into an HTML table.
2. A. Dreamweaver does not remove XML tags, if any, from Word documents.

12

1. B. The action attribute designates a program or script that can accept and process the submitted form data.
2. A and C. Form data can be passed on the URL (`GET`) or passed in the body (`POST`).

13

1. C. The `<noframes>` tag stores HTML that is shown on browsers or devices that are unable to process the `<frameset>` and `<frames>` tags.
2. A. A frameset file can be used as the source of a frame. This is one way of nesting framesets within each other.
3. B. Framesets can be used to pull together content from different servers into a single browser window. This cannot be done with any other HTML object.

14

1. B. The # sign is required to indicate an id.
2. C. Line 3 is missing a semicolon to separate it from the next property/value pair.

15

1. C. Pages are created from templates, so they cannot be dragged into an existing page.
2. B. False. It displays assets only from within the site for the document in the Document window.

16

1. B. The Library folder contains all of the library items available to you for a particular site.
2. C. An MXP file is a Macromedia extension package. Although it is created by using HTML and JavaScript, it is programmed to install itself through the Macromedia Extension Manager.
3. B. Whenever you modify a library item by renaming it or editing and saving it, Dreamweaver will ask if it can update all uses of the library item.

17

1. B and C. Either of these methods will work but have different consequences.
2. D. There is no limit to the number of templates you can define for a site.

18

1. A and D. The two valid types for server-side includes are File and Virtual. In general, File is used with Microsoft IIS and Virtual is used with Apache.
2. B. Server-side includes allow commonly used HTML to be stored in unique files which then can be inserted into other files by the Web server.

19

1. A. The "Show Events For" menu changes the browser level you are coding for, and as a result, changes the behavior options available to you.
2. B. `onMouseOver` and `onMouseLoad` are used to sense when the user's cursor is over the target graphic, so that JavaScript can be used to swap out the graphic.
3. C. Behaviors are written using the JavaScript language, which runs in all major browsers.

20

1. False. Design notes are stored in a separate file, so they will never be downloaded to the browser.
2. False. Check in/out is used only for single-thread access to a file by displaying checked out status in the Site window.

21

1. D. For `href` attributes pointing to JavaScript code, Dreamweaver does not check the validity of the script code.
2. C. Orphans are files that exist in the site directory structure but cannot be reached through links from any other page.

22

1. A. All remote access methods have a form of check in and check out.
2. D. The Local Root folder and the Host Directory should point to the same point in the structure of the site. In most cases, this is the site root.
3. A. Design notes can easily be shared by turning on a simple option.

INDEX

A

B

D

G

H

I

J

K-L

M

N

O

Q-R

S

T

U

V

W

X-Z